TOWER XPRESS AIR FRYER OVEN COOKBOOK:

*Healthy & Easy
Tower Air Fryer Recipes.*

By
Arthur Bradley

© Copyright by Arthur Bradley 2023 - All rights reserved.

The content contained within this book may not be reproduced, duplicated or transmitted without direct written permission from the author or the publisher.

Under no circumstances will any blame or legal responsibility be held against the publisher, or author, for any damages, reparation, or monetary loss due to the information contained within this book. Either directly or indirectly. You are responsible for your own choices, actions, and results.

Legal Notice:
This book is copyright protected. This book is only for personal use. You cannot amend, distribute, sell, use, quote or paraphrase any part, or the content within this book, without the consent of the author or publisher.

Disclaimer Notice:
Please note the information contained within this document is for educational and entertainment purposes only. All effort has been executed to present accurate, up to date, and reliable, complete information. No warranties of any kind are declared or implied. Readers acknowledge that the author is not engaging in the rendering of legal, financial, medical or professional advice. The content within this book has been derived from various sources. Please consult a licensed professional before attempting any techniques outlined in this book.

By reading this document, the reader agrees that under no circumstances is the author responsible for any losses, direct or indirect, which are incurred as a result of the use of the information contained within this document, including, but not limited to, — errors, omissions, or inaccuracies.

TABLE OF CONTENTS

INTRODUCTION
5

BREAKFAST RECIPES
11

LUNCH RECIPES
17

APPETIZERS AND SIDE DISHES
23

FISH AND SEAFOOD RECIPES
29

POULTRY RECIPES
35

MEAT RECIPES
46

VEGETABLE RECIPES
57

DESSERTS
63

CONCLUSION
69

INTRODUCTION

Are you ready to upgrade your cooking? I'm talking about a healthier way of making food that tastes even better than it looks. Then look no further than the Tower Xpress Air Fryer Oven Cookbook. It is the ultimate guide to making amazing meals and doing so with an air fryer.

This epic cookbook contains 100 delicious recipes that will make you salivate just by reading them. You will understand and respect food better when you use this cookbook. Crispy fries and juicy chicken are no match for this book; there are also amazing dessert recipes.

The Cookbook isn't just a collection of recipes. It is an invaluable resource that will help you understand the ins and outs of air frying. Learn about the unique features of your Tower Air Fryer Oven and discover innovative cooking methods that will maximize flavor and reduce oil usage.

Cooking is one thing, but air frying is just something else. This cookbook makes your cooking process faster and easier, with clear instructions and simple recipes. This cookbook will make your cooking experience more enjoyable and stress-free. It covers various recipe categories, from breakfast, lunch, and appetizers to desserts. Now, this book is an opportunity for you to impress your family and friends by making restaurant-level meals right in your kitchen.

If you are ready to take it up a notch and dive head first into the world of air frying, then the Tower Xpress Air Fryer Oven Cookbook is for you. Here lie mouthwatering flavors, healthier cooking options, and endless possibilities. Enjoy all of that from your own Tower Xpress Air Fryer Oven. So, thank you, and happy air frying!

Why use an Air Fryer?

There are several benefits and advantages to using an air fryer:

1. **Healthier Cooking Appliance:** Air fryers use a hot air circulation technique to cook food, requiring little or sometimes no oil. This means you can enjoy delicious and crispy dishes with very little fat content compared to traditional frying methods. It is one of the healthier options for those who want to reduce their daily calorie intake.

2. **Reduced Calorie Intake:** Air fryers require less oil or sometimes no oil to cook your food. It helps to reduce the calorie content of your favorite fried foods. It is one of the great ways to enjoy your favorite meals, such as fries, chicken wings, and more.

3. **Faster cooking:** Air fryers cook food using hot air, which cooks faster than traditional ovens or deep fryers. The hot air circulation technique in air fryers ensures food is cooked quickly and evenly in shorter cooking times. This can be especially beneficial for a person who has a busy schedule.

4. **Multifunctional:** Air fryers are not just for frying your food but also for grilling, roasting, baking, and dehydrating your food. This versatility allows you to prepare various dishes using a single appliance.

5. **Energy Efficient:** Air fryers typically use less energy compared with traditional ovens. They are compact, so they heat up quickly and require less power.

6. **Easy Cleanup:** Most Air fryer models are designed for easy cleaning; they come with dishwasher-safe and non-stick coatings that make cleaning a breeze. This saves you time and effort for the cleaning process.

7. **Safe to Use:** Air fryers are generally safe to use, with features like automatic shut-off timers and temperature controls. They work in a closed environment, reducing the risk of hot oil splatters and the chances of accidents in the kitchen.

How to use the Power Xpress air fryer?

The Power Xpress air fryer is an easy-to-use multifunctional cooking appliance. Follow the step-by-step instructions below to use your Power Xpress air fryer or similar model. Here are some general steps for using an air fryer.

1. *Preparation:*
- First, place your air fryer on a flat, stable, and heat-resistant surface, and ensure you have left enough space around the air fryer for air circulation and ventilation.
- Make sure all the air fryer parts are perfectly clean and dry before starting the cooking process.

2. *Power on air fryer:*
- Plug the air fryer power cord into a power socket and power it on using a power button and air fryer main control dial.

3. *Preheat:*
- It is important to preheat your air fryer to the desired temperature. Preheating allows the air fryer to reach the optimal cooking temperature, ensuring that you get even, crispy, and delicious cooking results. So, don't forget to preheat your fryer before you start cooking to enjoy your guilt-free meals.

4. *Prepare your food:*
- Proper food preparation involves seasoning, coating with oil or cooking spray (if needed), and arranging the food to allow optimal air circulation.

5. *Time and Temperature setting:*
- Set the desired time and temperature settings as per your recipe needs. This air fryer allows you to set times between 1 to 60 minutes and temperatures between 80°C and 200°C.

6. *Start cooking:*
- After setting the time and temperature settings, press the start button to start the cooking process.
- During the cooking process, flip your food if needed.

7. *Completion:*
- After cooking, safely remove your food from the air fryer with the help of a tong or spatula and serve.

8. *Cleaning:*
- Allow your air fryer to cool down before starting the cleaning process. Most air fryer parts, such as the cooking basket and drip tray, are usually dishwasher-safe.
- Wipe down the interior and exterior of the air fryer with the help of a clean, damp cloth.

Parts and Accessories

Tower Xpress Air Fryer comes with some common components you might find as follows.

1. **Main Unit:** This is the main body of your air fryer, which is equipped with the heating element, fan, and controls. The exterior of the air fryer is made of stainless steel and is also part of this unit.

2. **Cooking Tray or Basket:** The cooking tray or basket is where you place your favorite food for cooking. It is usually made of metal, has a non-stick coating to prevent sticking, and is easy to clean. Some other models come with a handle on the basket for easy removal.

3. **Drip Pan or tray:** It is situated below the cooking basket to catch any dripping or crumbs that fall during the cooking process. It helps to keep your air fryer clean and also prevents smoke.

4. **Divider or Separator:** Dividers or separators prevent mixing two foods during cooking. These are useful accessories for preparing multiple food items simultaneously.

5. **Grill Rack or Skewers:** A grill rack or skewers are used in an air fryer to hold food items such as kebabs, skewered vegetables, smaller pieces of meats, etc.

Features & Functions of Tower Xpress Air Fryer

Some of the features and functions of Tower Xpress Air Fryer may vary depending on its different model number, but here are some general functions and features usually found in air fryers:

1. **Air Fry:** This is one of the primary functions of an air fryer, which cooks food using a hot air circulation technique. It can crisp up your food, making it a healthier alternative than deep frying.

2. **Roast:** A roast function allows you to cook meat and vegetables, giving them a roasted-like texture and enhancing flavor.

3. **Grill:** Some air fryer models come with a grill function, which allows you to grill foods like burgers, vegetables, steaks, etc.

4. **Bake:** Air fryers can work as mini ovens and also allow you to bake cakes, cookies, muffins, and more.

5. **Dehydrating:** Dehydrating function allows you to preserve your food for a longer time. You can dry fruits, jerky, or many other snacks using this function and store them for longer.

6. **Temperature Control:** Your Tower Xpress Air Fryer allows you to set temperatures between 80°C and 200°C. You can choose a temperature from these ranges to achieve the desired level of doneness and crispiness for your food.

7. **Timer:** This function allows you to set the cooking time to 1 minute to 60 minutes and automatically turns off the appliance when the time reaches zero.

8. **Preheat:** Some air fryers come with a preheat function, which can be useful for specific recipes that benefit from a preheated cooking chamber.

9. **Keep Warm:** This function keeps your food warm after finishing your cooking process, which ensures food is ready to serve when you are ready to eat.

10. **Preset programs:** Some air fryer models have preset cooking programs for dishes like chicken, fries, fish, and more. These programs automatically set the time and temperature as per your recipe needs.

11. **Auto Shut-off:** This function allows your air fryer to turn off when the cooking cycle is complete automatically. This is one of the best security features for most air fryers.

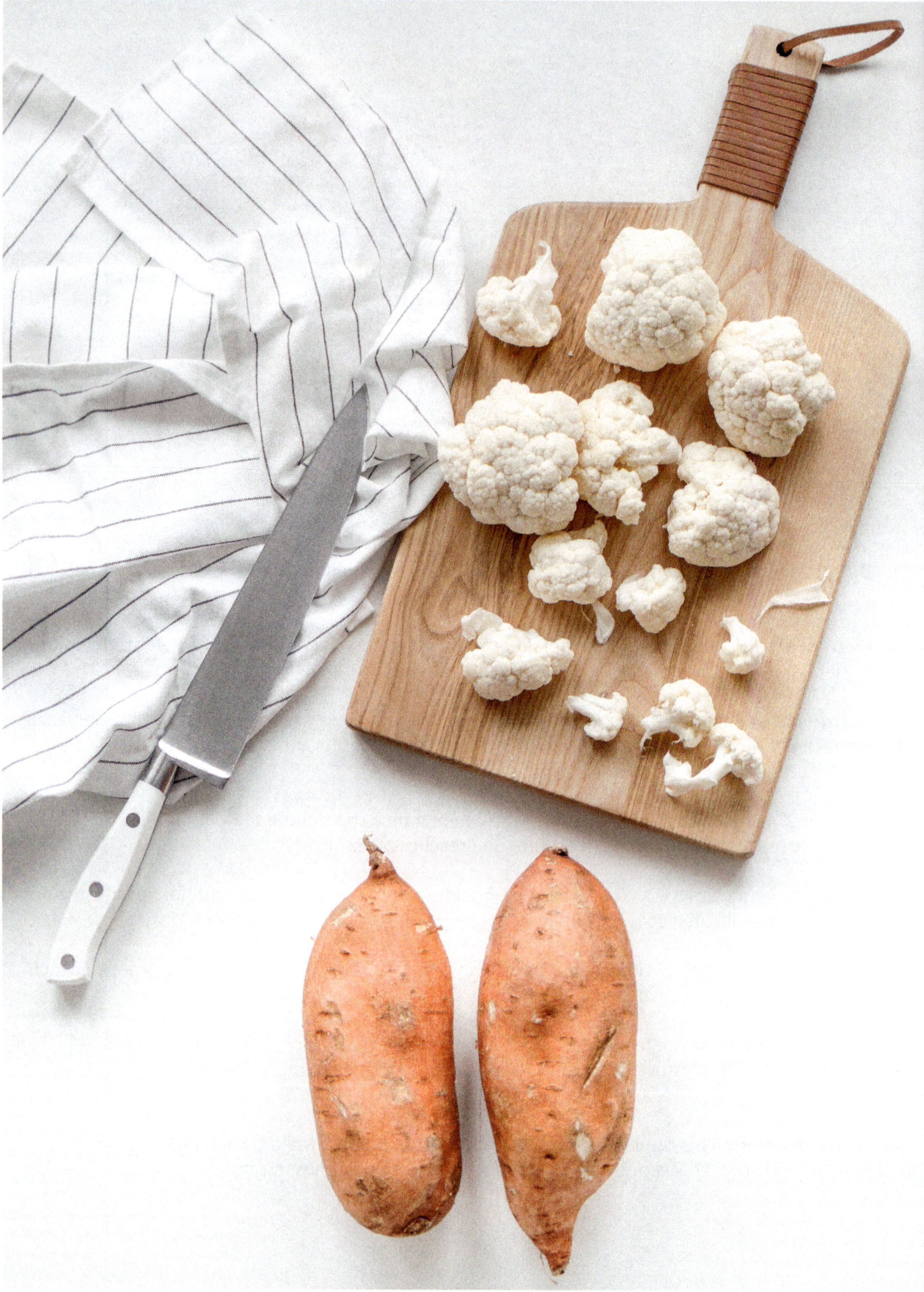

BREAKFAST RECIPES

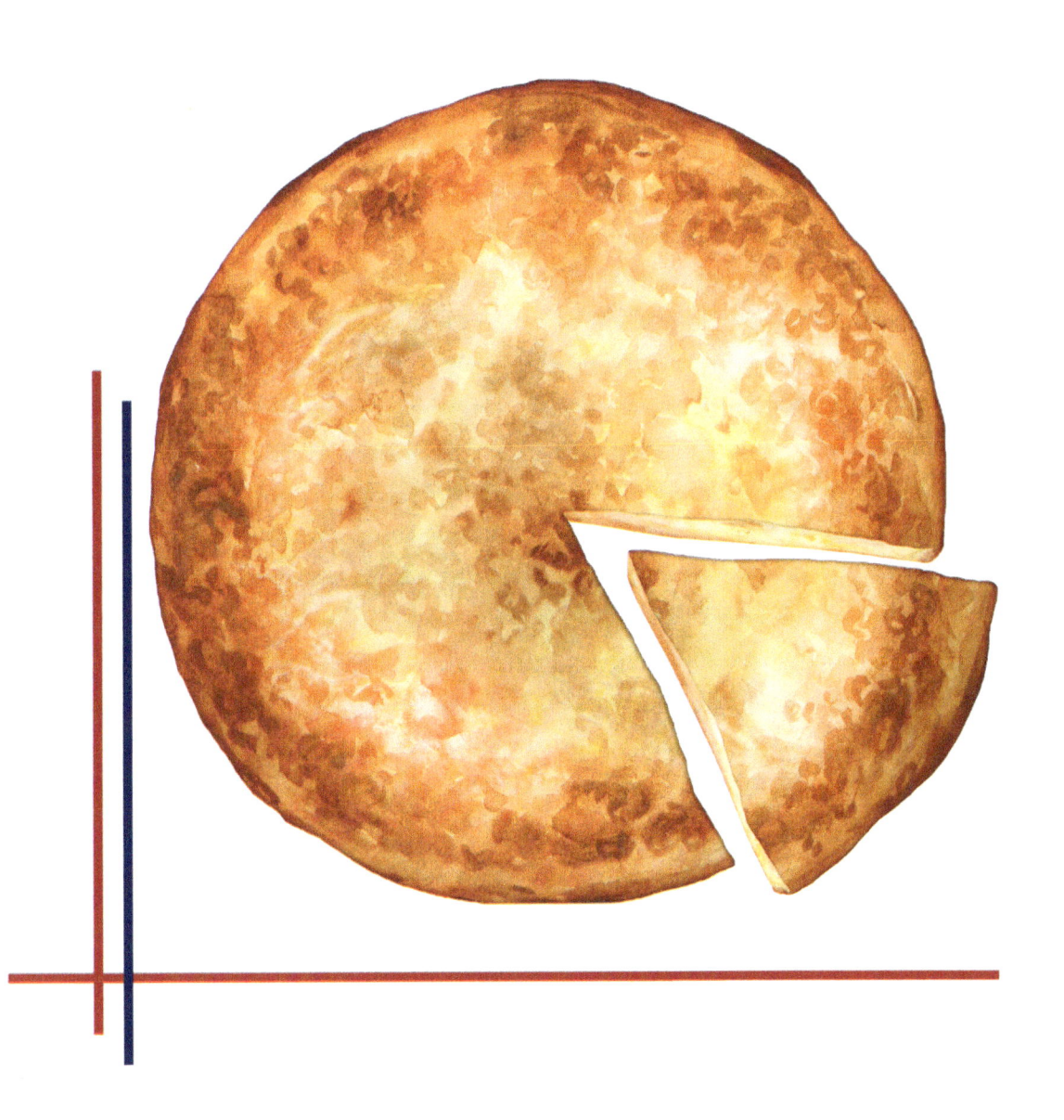

Healthy Egg Bite Cups

PER SERVING:
CALORIES 122, CARBS 1.5G, FAT 9G, PROTEIN 8G

COOK TIME: 09 MINUTES
SERVES: 6
INGREDIENTS:

- Eggs - 6
- Ground sausage, cooked - 1/4 cup
- Cheddar cheese, shredded - 1/2 cup
- Onions, diced - 1/4 cup
- Bell peppers, diced - 1/4 cup
- Heavy cream - 2 tbsp
- Pepper - To taste
- Salt - To taste

DIRECTIONS:

1. Whisk eggs with heavy cream, pepper, and salt in a mixing bowl.
2. Add cooked sausage, shredded cheese, onion, and bell peppers and stir well to combine.
3. Spray the muffin pan with cooking spray.
4. Pour the egg mixture into the prepared muffin pan and place the pan on the middle shelf of the air fryer.
5. Cook at 320 F/ 160 C for 6-9 minutes.
6. Serve and enjoy.

Vegetable Egg Bake

PER SERVING:
CALORIES 150, CARBS 4.7G, FAT 11G, PROTEIN 2G

COOK TIME: 35 MINUTES
SERVES: 12
INGREDIENTS:

- Eggs - 12
- Cherry tomatoes, chopped - 1 cup
- Bell pepper, diced - 1
- Small onion, diced - 1
- Olive oil - 1 tbsp
- Almond milk - 1 cup
- Feta cheese, crumbled - 1/2 cup
- Kale, chopped - 2 cups
- Pepper - To taste
- Salt - To taste

DIRECTIONS:

1. Preheat the air fryer to 400 F/ 204 C.
2. Heat oil in a pan over medium heat.
3. Add onion to the pan and sauté for 3 minutes.
4. Add bell pepper and cook for a minute. Remove pan from heat.
5. In a bowl, whisk eggs with milk, pepper, and salt.
6. Add sautéed onion and pepper and stir well.
7. Add feta cheese, kale, and tomatoes and stir until well combined.
8. Pour the egg mixture into the greased baking dish, place the baking dish on the bottom shelf of the air fryer, and bake for 30 minutes.
9. Slice and serve.

Spinach Breakfast Bake

PER SERVING:
CALORIES 208, CARBS 4G, FAT 14G, PROTEIN 15G

COOK TIME: 30 MINUTES
SERVES: 4
INGREDIENTS:

- Eggs - 10
- Garlic, minced - 1/2 tsp
- Sun-dried tomatoes, diced - 1/4 cup
- Bell peppers, diced - 1/2 cup
- Green onions, chopped - 1/4 cup
- Mozzarella cheese, shredded - 1/4 cup
- Parmesan cheese, shredded - 2 tbsp
- Almond milk - 1/4 cup
- Pepper - 1/2 tsp
- Baby spinach, chopped - 1 1/2 cups
- Salt - To taste

DIRECTIONS:

1. Preheat the air fryer to 375 F/ 190 C.
2. Spray the baking dish with cooking spray and set aside.
3. Whisk eggs with milk, pepper, and salt in a large bowl.
4. Add remaining ingredients and stir until well combined.
5. Pour the egg mixture into the baking dish, place the baking dish on the bottom shelf of the air fryer, and bake for 30 minutes.
6. Slice and serve.

Kale Zucchini Breakfast Bake

PER SERVING:
CALORIES 302, CARBS 8G, FAT 23G, PROTEIN 17G

COOK TIME: 30 MINUTES
SERVES: 4
INGREDIENTS:

- Eggs - 6
- Cheddar cheese, shredded - 1 cup
- Zucchini, shredded & squeezed - 1 cup
- Kale, chopped - 1 cup
- Onion, chopped - 1
- Almond flour - 1/2 cup
- Almond milk - 1/2 cup
- Dill - 1/2 tsp
- Oregano - 1/2 tsp
- Basil - 1/2 tsp
- Baking powder - 1/2 tsp
- Pepper - 1/4 tsp
- Salt - 1/4 tsp

DIRECTIONS:

1. Preheat the air fryer to 375 F/ 190 C.
2. Spray a 9*9-inch baking dish with cooking spray and set aside.
3. In a bowl, whisk eggs with milk, pepper, and salt.
4. Add remaining ingredients and stir until well combined.
5. Pour the egg mixture into the prepared baking dish, place the dish on the bottom shelf of the air fryer, and bake for 30 minutes.
6. Slice and serve.

Jalapeno Egg Muffins

PER SERVING:
CALORIES 96, CARBS 1.6G, FAT 7G, PROTEIN 6.2G

COOK TIME: 15 MINUTES
SERVES: 12
INGREDIENTS:

- Eggs - 10
- Bacon, cooked & crumbled - 1/3 cup
- Cheddar cheese, shredded - 1/2 cup
- Cream cheese, softened - 1/3 cup
- Jalapeno peppers, de-seeded & chopped - 3
- Onion powder - 1/2 tsp
- Garlic powder - 1/2 tsp
- Pepper - To taste
- Salt - To taste

DIRECTIONS:

1. Preheat the air fryer to 400 F/ 204 C.
2. Spray the muffin pan with cooking spray and set aside.
3. Whisk together eggs, garlic powder, onion powder, pepper, and salt in a mixing bowl.
4. Add bacon, cheese, cream cheese, and jalapeno peppers and stir until well combined.
5. Pour egg mixture into the prepared muffin pan, place the pan on the air fryer's middle shelf, and cook for 15 minutes.
6. Serve and enjoy.

Pumpkin Oatmeal

PER SERVING:
CALORIES 368, CARBS 32G, FAT 24G, PROTEIN 7G

COOK TIME: 30 MINUTES
SERVES: 6
INGREDIENTS:

- Rolled oats - 2 cups
- Maple syrup - 4 tbsp
- Canned pumpkin puree - 1 cup
- Almond milk - 1 1/2 cups
- Cinnamon - 1/2 tsp
- Walnuts, chopped - 1/2 cup
- Vanilla - 1 tsp
- Butter, melted - 1 tbsp
- Ground flaxseed - 1 tbsp
- Pumpkin pie spice - 1 tsp
- Baking powder - 1 tsp
- Sea salt - 1/2 tsp

DIRECTIONS:

1. Preheat the air fryer to 375 F/ 190 C.
2. Spray 8-inch baking pan with cooking spray and set aside.
3. Mix oats, baking powder, cinnamon, pumpkin pie spice, and salt in a bowl.
4. Add milk, vanilla, butter, flaxseed, maple syrup, and pumpkin puree and stir until well combined.
5. Add walnuts and stir until well combined.
6. Pour the oatmeal mixture into the prepared pan, place the pan on the air fryer's bottom shelf, and bake for 30-35 minutes.
7. Remove the baking pan from the oven and let it cool for 10 minutes.
8. Serve and enjoy.

Tater Tot Spinach Casserole

PER SERVING:
CALORIES 264, CARBS 15G, FAT 16G, PROTEIN 12G

COOK TIME: 40 MINUTES
SERVES: 8
INGREDIENTS:

- Eggs - 8
- Spinach, cooked until wilted - 4 oz
- Roasted red peppers, chopped - 2/3 cup
- Frozen tater tots - 16 oz
- Cheddar cheese, shredded - 1 1/2 cups
- Pepper - 1/4 tsp
- Salt - 1/4 tsp

DIRECTIONS:

1. Preheat the air fryer to 350 F/ 176 C.
2. In a bowl, whisk eggs with pepper and salt.
3. Add roasted peppers, spinach, and cheese and stir until well combined.
4. Arrange tater tots into the greased 11*7-inch baking dish.
5. Pour egg mixture over tater tots. Place the baking dish on the middle shelf of the air fryer and bake for 40 minutes.
6. Slice and serve.

Easy Cornbread

PER SERVING:
CALORIES 226, CARBS 36G, FAT 8G, PROTEIN 3G

COOK TIME: 10 MINUTES
SERVES: 9
INGREDIENTS:

- All-purpose flour - 1 1/4 cups
- Sugar - 1/3 cup
- Yellow cornmeal - 1 cup
- Applesauce - 1/3 cup
- Almond milk - 1 1/4 cups
- Baking powder - 1 tbsp
- Salt - 1 tsp

DIRECTIONS:

1. Mix flour, baking powder, cornmeal, sugar, and salt in a bowl.
2. Add milk and applesauce and mix until well combined.
3. Pour batter into the greased muffin pan.
4. Place the muffin pan on the bottom shelf of the air fryer and bake at 400 F/ 204 C for 10 minutes.
5. Serve and enjoy.

Banana Bread

PER SERVING:
CALORIES 140, CARBS 19G, FAT 5.9G, PROTEIN 2.5G

COOK TIME: 35 MINUTES
SERVES: 10
INGREDIENTS:
- Eggs, lightly beaten - 2
- Mashed banana - 1 cup
- Baking soda - 1/4 tsp
- Baking powder - 1/2 tsp
- All-purpose flour - 1 cup
- Vanilla - 1 tsp
- Butter, melted - 1/4 cup
- Sugar - 1/3 cup
- Salt - 1/4 tsp

DIRECTIONS:
1. Preheat the air fryer to 325 F/ 162 C.
2. Mix flour, baking powder, baking soda, sugar, and salt in a bowl.
3. Whisk eggs with butter, vanilla, and bananas in a separate bowl until well blended.
4. Add flour mixture into the egg mixture and mix until well combined.
5. Pour batter into the greased loaf pan, place the pan on the air fryer's bottom shelf, and bake for 35 minutes.
6. Slice and serve.

Healthy Breakfast Frittata

PER SERVING:
CALORIES 207, CARBS 5G, FAT 13G, PROTEIN 15G

COOK TIME: 16 MINUTES
SERVES: 2
INGREDIENTS:
- Eggs - 4
- Spring onion, chopped - 2
- Feta cheese, crumbled - 2 tbsp
- Cheddar cheese, grated - 2 tbsp
- Milk - 1/4 cup
- Fresh herbs, chopped - 1 tbsp
- Spinach, chopped - 1/4 cup
- Tomato, chopped - 1
- Pepper - To taste
- Salt - To taste

DIRECTIONS:
1. Preheat the air fryer to 350 F/ 176 C.
2. In a bowl, whisk eggs with milk, pepper, and salt.
3. Add spring onion, tomatoes, feta cheese, fresh herbs, spinach, and cheddar cheese, and stir well.
4. Pour the egg mixture into the greased air fryer baking pan, place the pan on the bottom shelf, and bake for 12-16 minutes.
5. Serve and enjoy.

LUNCH RECIPES

Carrots & Sweet Potatoes

PER SERVING:
CALORIES 375, CARBS 74G, FAT 7.3G, PROTEIN 4.7G

COOK TIME: 35 MINUTES
SERVES: 4
INGREDIENTS:

- Sweet potatoes, clean & cut into ½-inch cubes - 2 lbs
- Olive oil - 2 tbsp
- Carrots, clean & cut into ½-inch slices - 1 lb
- Onion powder - 1/4 tsp
- Paprika - 1/4 tsp
- Garlic cloves, minced - 1 tsp
- Pepper - To taste
- Salt - To taste

DIRECTIONS:

1. Preheat the air fryer to 400 F/ 204 C.
2. Add sweet potatoes, carrots, onion powder, paprika, garlic, oil, pepper, and salt in a bowl and toss until well coated.
3. Spread sweet potatoes and carrots onto an airflow rack lined with parchment paper on the middle shelf of the air fryer and air fry for 35-40 minutes.
4. Serve and enjoy.

Salmon Steak

PER SERVING:
CALORIES 322, CARBS 8G, FAT 20G, PROTEIN 22G

COOK TIME: 20 MINUTES
SERVES: 2
INGREDIENTS:

- Salmon steaks - 2
- Rice vinegar - 2 tbsp
- Worcestershire sauce - 3 tbsp
- Sesame oil - 2 tbsp
- Ginger garlic paste - 1 tbsp
- Pepper - To taste
- Salt - To taste

DIRECTIONS:

1. Add salmon steaks and remaining ingredients into the zip-lock bag. Seal the bag and place it in the refrigerator overnight.
2. Remove salmon steaks from the marinade and place them onto an airflow rack lined with parchment paper on the middle shelf of the air fryer.
3. Cook on air fry mode at 400 F/ 204 C for 20 minutes.
4. Serve and enjoy.

Juicy Turkey Breast

PER SERVING:
CALORIES 320, CARBS 23G, FAT 7G, PROTEIN 39G

COOK TIME: 37 MINUTES
SERVES: 4
INGREDIENTS:

- Turkey breast - 2 lbs
- Fresh sage, chopped - 1 tsp
- Fresh rosemary, chopped - 1 tsp
- Fresh thyme, chopped - 1 tsp
- Butter, melted - 1 tbsp
- Dijon mustard - 2 tbsp
- Maple syrup - 1/4 cup
- Pepper - To taste
- Salt - To taste

DIRECTIONS:

1. Mix thyme, rosemary, sage, pepper, and salt in a small bowl.
2. Rub turkey breast with herb mixture and place onto an airflow rack lined with parchment paper on the middle shelf of the air fryer.
3. Cook on air fry mode at 390 F/ 198 C for 30-35 minutes.
4. Mix butter, Dijon mustard, and maple syrup in a small bowl.
5. Brush the butter mixture all over the turkey breast.
6. Return turkey breast onto air flow rack and cook at 330 F/ 165 C for 2 minutes.
7. Slice and serve.

Tasty Shrimp Fajitas

PER SERVING:
CALORIES 270, CARBS 18G, FAT 9G, PROTEIN 27G

COOK TIME: 15 MINUTES
SERVES: 4
INGREDIENTS:

- Shrimp, peeled & deveined - 1 lb
- Poblano pepper, chopped - 1
- Bell peppers, sliced - 2
- Olive oil - 2 tbsp
- Orange juice - 1/2 cup
- Smoked paprika - 2 tsp
- Fajita seasoning - 3 tbsp
- Onion, sliced - 1
- Fresh lime juice - 1/4 cup
- Salt - To taste

DIRECTIONS:

1. In a mixing bowl, mix shrimp and remaining ingredients. Cover and place in refrigerator for 1 hour.
2. Preheat the air fryer to 400 F/ 204 C.
3. Add shrimp and vegetables onto an airflow rack lined with parchment paper on the middle shelf of the air fryer and cook for 15 minutes.
4. Serve and enjoy.

Salmon with Vegetables

PER SERVING:
CALORIES 420, CARBS 29G, FAT 18G, PROTEIN 39G

COOK TIME: 12 MINUTES
SERVES: 2
INGREDIENTS:

- Salmon fillets - 2
- Yellow bell pepper, sliced - 1
- Green bell pepper, sliced - 1
- Carrot, chopped - 1
- Red bell pepper, sliced - 1
- Green beans, chopped - 5
- Celery stalk, chopped - 1
- Olive oil - 1 tbsp
- Onion powder - 1 tsp
- Garlic powder - 1 tsp
- Cayenne pepper - 1 tsp
- Pepper - To taste
- Salt - To taste

DIRECTIONS:

1. Mix onion powder, pepper, garlic powder, cayenne, and salt in a small bowl and rub over salmon fillets.
2. Place salmon fillets into the greased baking dish.
3. Add vegetables around the salmon fillets. Drizzle with olive oil.
4. Place the baking dish on the middle shelf of the air fryer and cook at 350 F/ 176 C for 12 minutes.
5. Serve and enjoy.

Lemon Caper Fish Fillets

PER SERVING:
CALORIES 173, CARBS 0.7G, FAT 9.9G, PROTEIN 20G

COOK TIME: 10 MINUTES
SERVES: 2
INGREDIENTS:

- Cod fillets - 2
- Butter, melted - 1 1/2 tbsp
- Fresh lemon juice - 3 tbsp
- Lemon zest, grated - 1/2 tsp
- Caper - 1 tbsp
- Pepper - To taste
- Salt - To taste

DIRECTIONS:

1. Season cod fillets with pepper and salt and place into the greased baking pan.
2. Place the baking pan on the middle shelf of the air fryer and cook at 360 F/ 182 C for 6 minutes.
3. Mix lemon juice, caper, butter, and lemon zest in a small bowl and pour over cod fillets.
4. Cook cod fillets for 4 minutes more.
5. Serve and enjoy.

Simple Chicken Thighs

PER SERVING:
CALORIES 230, CARBS 0.7G, FAT 9G, PROTEIN 33G

COOK TIME: 12 MINUTES
SERVES: 8
INGREDIENTS:

- Chicken thighs, boneless & skinless - 2 lbs
- Ground cumin - 1 tsp
- Chili powder - 2 tsp
- Garlic powder - 1 tsp
- Olive oil - 2 tsp
- Pepper - To taste
- Salt - To taste

DIRECTIONS:

1. Mix chicken with oil, garlic powder, pepper, chili powder, cumin, and salt in a mixing bowl until well coated.
2. Place chicken onto an airflow rack lined with parchment paper on the middle shelf of the air fryer.
3. Cook on air fry mode at 400 F/ 204 C for 12 minutes.
4. Serve and enjoy.

Curried Chicken Skewers

PER SERVING:
CALORIES 540, CARBS 16G, FAT 20.8G, PROTEIN 70G

COOK TIME: 15 MINUTES
SERVES: 4
INGREDIENTS:

- Chicken thighs, cut into cubes - 2 lbs
- Fresh lime juice - 3 tbsp
- Coconut milk - 1/4 cup
- Tamari soy sauce - 1/2 cup
- Thai red curry - 2 tbsp
- Maple syrup - 3 tbsp

DIRECTIONS:

1. Add chicken and remaining ingredients into the mixing bowl and mix well. Cover and place in refrigerator for 2 hours.
2. Thread marinated chicken onto the soaked skewers.
3. Place chicken skewers onto an airflow rack lined with parchment paper on the middle shelf of the air fryer.
4. Cook on air fry mode at 350 F/ 176 C for 15 minutes.
5. Serve and enjoy.

Marinated Chicken Bites

PER SERVING:
CALORIES 495, CARBS 1G, FAT 23G, PROTEIN 65G

COOK TIME: 20 MINUTES
SERVES: 4
INGREDIENTS:

- Chicken thighs, cut into chunks - 2 lbs
- White pepper - 1/4 tsp
- Onion powder - 1/2 tsp
- Olive oil - 2 tbsp
- Fresh lemon juice - 1/4 cup
- Garlic powder - 1/2 tsp
- Pepper - To taste
- Salt - To taste

DIRECTIONS:

1. Add chicken chunks and remaining ingredients into the large bowl and mix well. Cover and place in refrigerator for overnight.
2. Place marinated chicken onto an airflow rack lined with parchment paper on the middle shelf of the air fryer.
3. Cook on air fry mode at 380 F/ 193 C for 20 minutes.
4. Serve and enjoy.

Chipotle Pork Chops

PER SERVING:
CALORIES 305, CARBS 4G, FAT 23G, PROTEIN 18G

COOK TIME: 12 MINUTES
SERVES: 4
INGREDIENTS:

- Pork chops, boneless - 4
- Garlic powder - 2 tsp
- Chipotle chili powder - 1 tbsp
- Olive oil - 1 tbsp
- Onion powder - 2 tsp
- Pepper - To taste
- Salt - To taste

DIRECTIONS:

1. Preheat the air fryer to 400 F/ 204 C.
2. Mix chili powder, onion powder, garlic powder, pepper, and salt in a small bowl.
3. Brush pork chops with oil and rub with spice mixture.
4. Place pork chops onto an airflow rack lined with parchment paper on the middle shelf of the air fryer and cook for 12 minutes.
5. Serve and enjoy.

APPETIZERS AND SIDE DISHES

Salsa Cheese Dip

PER SERVING:
CALORIES 328, CARBS 3.8G, FAT 29G, PROTEIN 12.5G

COOK TIME: 30 MINUTES
SERVES: 10
INGREDIENTS:

- Cream cheese, softened - 14 oz
- Chunky salsa - 1/2 cup
- Paprika - 1/4 tsp
- Sour cream - 1 cup
- Cheddar cheese, shredded - 3 cups
- Pepper - To taste
- Salt - To taste

DIRECTIONS:

1. Preheat the air fryer to 350 F/ 176 C.
2. Mix all ingredients until well combined in a bowl and pour into the greased baking dish.
3. Place the baking dish on the bottom shelf of the air fryer and cook on bake mode for 30 minutes.
4. Serve and enjoy.

Garlic Goat's Cheese Dip

PER SERVING:
CALORIES 275, CARBS 2G, FAT 23G, PROTEIN 14G

COOK TIME: 20 MINUTES
SERVES: 8
INGREDIENTS:

- Goat's cheese - 12 oz
- Olive oil - 2 tbsp
- Parmesan cheese, shredded - 1/2 cup
- Cream cheese - 4 oz
- Rosemary, chopped - 2 tsp
- Red pepper flakes - 1 tsp
- Garlic cloves, minced - 4
- Salt - 1/2 tsp

DIRECTIONS:

1. Preheat the air fryer to 390 F/ 198 C.
2. Add all ingredients into the bowl and mix until well combined.
3. Pour the mixture into the greased baking dish and place the baking dish on the bottom shelf of the air fryer.
4. Bake for 20 minutes.
5. Serve and enjoy.

Spicy Lemon Chickpeas

PER SERVING:
CALORIES 220, CARBS 24G, FAT 11G, PROTEIN 5G

COOK TIME: 30 MINUTES
SERVES: 4
INGREDIENTS:

- Chickpeas, drained - 15 oz can
- Fresh lemon juice - 1 tbsp
- Olive oil - 3 tbsp
- Cayenne - 1/8 tsp
- Smoked paprika - 1/2 tsp
- Garlic powder - 1/2 tsp
- Pepper - To taste
- Salt - To taste

DIRECTIONS:

1. Preheat the air fryer to 400 F/ 204 C.
2. Add chickpeas and remaining ingredients into the mixing bowl and toss well.
3. Spread chickpeas onto an airflow rack lined with parchment paper on the middle shelf of the air fryer and cook for 25-30 minutes.
4. Serve and enjoy.

Garlic Rosemary Mushrooms

PER SERVING:
CALORIES 27, CARBS 4.1G, FAT 0.4G, PROTEIN 3G

COOK TIME: 14 MINUTES
SERVES: 4
INGREDIENTS:

- Mushroom caps - 1 lb
- Basil, minced - 1 tbsp
- Garlic clove, minced - 1
- Ground coriander - 1/2 tsp
- Rosemary, chopped - 1 tsp
- Vinegar - 1/2 tbsp
- Pepper - To taste
- Salt - To taste

DIRECTIONS:

1. Preheat the air fryer to 350 F/ 176 C.
2. Add all ingredients into the mixing bowl and toss well.
3. Add mushroom mixture onto the airflow rack lined with parchment paper on the middle shelf of the air fryer.
4. Cook mushrooms on air fry mode for 14 minutes
5. Serve and enjoy.

Spicy Tofu

PER SERVING:
CALORIES 175, CARBS 2G, FAT 14.4G, PROTEIN 11G

COOK TIME: 15 MINUTES
SERVES: 4
INGREDIENTS:

- Extra-firm tofu, pressed & cut into cubes - 1 lb
- Olive oil - 2 tbsp
- Sambal oelek paste - 2 tbsp
- Sesame oil - 1 tsp
- Soy sauce - 1 tbsp
- Salt - 1/8 tsp

DIRECTIONS:

1. Toss tofu cubes with soy sauce, olive oil, sesame oil, sambal oelek paste, and salt until well coated.
2. Spread tofu cubes onto an airflow rack lined with parchment paper on the middle shelf of the air fryer.
3. Cook tofu on air fry mode at 375 F/ 190 C for 15 minutes.
4. Serve and enjoy.

Tasty Cabbage Patties

PER SERVING:
CALORIES 55, CARBS 3G, FAT 4.2G, PROTEIN 2.2G

COOK TIME: 14 MINUTES
SERVES: 4
INGREDIENTS:

- Egg - 1
- Cabbage, grated - 1 1/2 cups
- Cilantro, minced - 1 tbsp
- Onion, chopped - 1 tbsp
- Ground cumin - 1 tsp
- Coconut flour - 1 tbsp
- Garlic clove, minced - 1
- Olive oil - 2 tsp
- Salt - 1/2 tsp

DIRECTIONS:

1. Add grated cabbage and remaining ingredients in a bowl and mix until well combined.
2. Make patties from the cabbage mixture and place them onto an airflow rack lined with parchment paper on the middle shelf of the air fryer.
3. Cook patties on air fry mode at 350 F/ 176 C for 14 minutes.
4. Serve and enjoy.

Savory Walnuts

PER SERVING:
CALORIES 173, CARBS 27.3G, FAT 7.6G, PROTEIN 1.5G

COOK TIME: 10 MINUTES
SERVES: 2
INGREDIENTS:

- Walnut halves - 1 cup
- Sesame seeds - 2 tbsp
- Cayenne - 1/4 tsp
- Ground cumin - 1/4 tsp
- Butter - 1/2 tbsp
- Water - 1 tbsp
- Sugar - 1/4 cup
- White pepper powder - 1/4 tsp
- Salt - 1/4 tsp

DIRECTIONS:

1. Add butter, cumin, sugar, water, cayenne, white pepper powder, and salt into the bowl and microwave for 1 minute.
2. Add walnuts and sesame seeds into the bowl and toss until well coated.
3. Spread walnuts onto an airflow rack lined with parchment paper on the middle shelf of the air fryer.
4. Cook on air fry mode at 300 F/ 148 C for 10 minutes.
5. Serve and enjoy.

Crispy Sweet Potato Fries

PER SERVING:
CALORIES 112, CARBS 18G, FAT 3.7G, PROTEIN 2.9G

COOK TIME: 25 MINUTES
SERVES: 4
INGREDIENTS:

- Sweet potato, cut into fries' shape - 12 oz
- Ground ginger - 1/2 tsp
- Garlic powder - 1 tsp
- Ground coriander - 1/2 tsp
- Olive oil - 1 tbsp
- Paprika - 1 tsp
- Salt - To taste

DIRECTIONS:

1. In a bowl, toss sweet potato fries with oil.
2. Spread sweet potato fries onto an airflow rack lined with parchment paper on the middle shelf of the air fryer.
3. Cook on air fry mode at 400 F/ 200 C for 18 minutes.
4. Toss sweet potato fries with spices, return to airflow rack, and cook for 6 more minutes.
5. Serve and enjoy.

Crunchy & Savory Almonds

PER SERVING:
CALORIES 183, CARBS 8G, FAT 16G, PROTEIN 5G

COOK TIME: 06 MINUTES
SERVES: 4
INGREDIENTS:

- Almonds - 1 cup
- Olive oil - 1 tbsp
- Cumin - 1 tsp
- Chili powder - 2 tsp
- Garlic powder - 1 tsp
- Onion powder - 1 tsp
- Smoked paprika - 1 tbsp
- Salt - To taste

DIRECTIONS:

1. Add almonds and remaining ingredients into the bowl and toss until well coated.
2. Spread almonds onto an airflow rack lined with parchment paper on the middle shelf of the air fryer.
3. Cook on air fry mode at 320 F/ 160 C for 6 minutes.
4. Serve and enjoy.

Sweet Potato Wedges

PER SERVING:
CALORIES 116, CARBS 12G, FAT 7.2G, PROTEIN 1.5G

COOK TIME: 20 MINUTES
SERVES: 2
INGREDIENTS:

- Sweet potato, cut into wedges - 1
- Garlic powder - 1/2 tsp
- Paprika - 1/2 tsp
- Cayenne - 1/8 tsp
- Olive oil - 1 tbsp
- Pepper - To taste
- Salt - To taste

DIRECTIONS:

1. Toss sweet potato wedges with oil, paprika, garlic powder, cayenne, pepper, and salt in a bowl.
2. Add sweet potato wedges onto the airflow rack lined with parchment paper on the middle shelf of the air fryer.
3. Cook on air fry mode at 400 F/ 204 C for 20 minutes.
4. Serve and enjoy.

FISH AND SEAFOOD RECIPES

Delicious Asian Salmon

PER SERVING:
CALORIES 366, CARBS 25G, FAT 14G, PROTEIN 33.7G

COOK TIME: 08 MINUTES
SERVES: 4
INGREDIENTS:

- Salmon fillets - 4
- Lemon pepper - 1/4 tsp
- Cold water - 1 1/2 tsp
- Cornstarch - 1 1/2 tsp
- Garlic, minced - 1 tsp
- Sesame oil - 1/4 tsp
- Rice vinegar - 1 1/2 tsp
- Honey - 1/3 cup
- Soy sauce, low-sodium - 2 1/2 tbsp
- Olive oil - 1 tbsp

DIRECTIONS:

1. Preheat the air fryer to 400 F/ 204 C.
2. Brush salmon fillets with olive oil and place them onto an airflow rack lined with parchment paper on the middle shelf of the air fryer and cook for 8 minutes.
3. Mix soy sauce, water, cornstarch, garlic, sesame oil, vinegar, and honey in a small saucepan and cook over medium heat until reduced and thickened.
4. Brush cooked salmon, top with sauce, and sprinkle with lemon pepper.
5. Serve and enjoy.

White Fish Fillets

PER SERVING:
CALORIES 165, CARBS 2.1G, FAT 8G, PROTEIN 18.8G

COOK TIME: 15 MINUTES
SERVES: 4
INGREDIENTS:

- White fish fillets - 1 lb
- Ground cumin - 1/2 tsp
- Chili powder - 1 tsp
- Onion powder - 2 tsp
- Dried oregano, crushed - 1 tbsp
- Pepper
- Salt

DIRECTIONS:

1. Preheat the air fryer to 350 F/ 176 C.
2. Mix cumin, oregano, pepper, onion powder, chili powder, and salt in a small bowl.
3. Rub fish fillets with the spice mixture.
4. Place fish fillets onto an airflow rack lined with parchment paper on the middle shelf of the air fryer and bake for 15 minutes.
5. Serve and enjoy.

Orange Honey Salmon

PER SERVING:
CALORIES 395, CARBS 23.2G, FAT 14.2G, PROTEIN 45.7G

COOK TIME: 25 MINUTES
SERVES: 2
INGREDIENTS:

- Salmon fillets - 1 lb
- Orange zest, grated - 1
- Honey - 2 tbsp
- Orange juice - 1
- Soy sauce - 3 tbsp

DIRECTIONS:

1. Preheat the air fryer to 400 F/ 204 C.
2. Mix honey, soy sauce, orange juice, and orange zest in a small bowl.
3. Place salmon fillets in a baking dish and pour the honey mixture over the fish fillets.
4. Place the baking dish on the bottom shelf of the air fryer and bake for 25 minutes.
5. Serve and enjoy.

Flavorful Mahi-Mahi Fish Fillets

PER SERVING:
CALORIES 123, CARBS 2.5G, FAT 10.4G, PROTEIN 5.1G

COOK TIME: 12 MINUTES
SERVES: 4
INGREDIENTS:

- Mahi Mahi fish fillets - 4
- Smoked paprika - 1 tsp
- Cayenne - 1/2 tsp
- Garlic powder - 1/2 tsp
- Olive oil - 3 tbsp
- Oregano - 1 tsp
- Ground cumin - 3/4 tsp
- Onion powder - 1 tsp
- Pepper
- Salt

DIRECTIONS:

1. Preheat the air fryer to 400 F/ 204 C.
2. Mix cayenne, oregano, paprika, onion powder, cumin, garlic powder, pepper, and salt in a small bowl.
3. Place fish fillets in a baking dish, drizzle with oil and sprinkle with spice mixture.
4. Place the baking dish on the bottom shelf of the air fryer and Bake for 12 minutes.
5. Serve and enjoy.

Greek Shrimp

PER SERVING:
CALORIES 184, CARBS 6G, FAT 5G, PROTEIN 26.1G

COOK TIME: 25 MINUTES
SERVES: 4
INGREDIENTS:

- Shrimp, peeled - 1 lb
- Garlic, sliced - 1 tbsp
- Grape tomatoes - 2 cups
- Italian seasoning - 1/2 tsp
- Olive oil - 1 tbsp
- Pepper
- Salt

DIRECTIONS:
1. Preheat the air fryer to 400 F/ 204 C.
2. Add shrimp and remaining ingredients into the bowl and toss well.
3. Transfer the shrimp mixture to the baking dish.
4. Place the baking dish on the bottom shelf of the air fryer and bake for 25 minutes.
5. Serve and enjoy.

Shrimp Skewers

PER SERVING:
CALORIES 70, CARBS 1.3G, FAT 1.2G, PROTEIN 11G

COOK TIME: 08 MINUTES
SERVES: 2
INGREDIENTS:

- Frozen shrimp, thawed - 1 cup
- Lemon juice - 1
- Garlic clove, minced - 1
- Paprika - 1/4 tsp
- Ground black pepper - 1/4 tsp
- Salt - 1/8 tsp

DIRECTIONS:
1. Preheat the air fryer to 350 F/ 180 C.
2. Toss shrimp with paprika, pepper, lemon juice, garlic, and salt in a bowl.
3. Thread shrimp onto the soaked skewers and place them onto an airflow rack lined with parchment paper on the middle shelf of the air fryer.
4. Cook on air fry mode for 8 minutes.
5. Serve and enjoy.

Fish Skewers

PER SERVING:
CALORIES 140, CARBS 15G, FAT 3G, PROTEIN 16G

COOK TIME: 10 MINUTES
SERVES: 2
INGREDIENTS:

- Swordfish steak, cut into chunks - 1
- Bell pepper, cut into pieces - 1
- Zucchini, cut into pieces - 1
- Onion, cut into pieces - 1
- Pepper
- Salt

DIRECTIONS:

1. Season fish chunks with pepper and salt.
2. Thread fish chunks, onion, bell pepper, and zucchini pieces onto the soaked skewers.
3. Place fish skewers onto an airflow rack lined with parchment paper on the middle shelf of the air fryer.
4. Cook on air fry mode at 375 F/ 190 C for 10 minutes.
5. Serve and enjoy.

Spicy Asian Shrimp Skewers

PER SERVING:
CALORIES 117, CARBS 8G, FAT 3.4G, PROTEIN 14.8G

COOK TIME: 08 MINUTES
SERVES: 8
INGREDIENTS:

- Shrimp, peeled & deveined - 1 lb
- Korean gochujang - 1 tbsp
- Honey - 1 tbsp
- Soy sauce - 1 tbsp
- Olive oil - 1/2 tbsp
- Garlic, minced - 1/2 tsp
- Fresh lemon juice - 1/2 tbsp

DIRECTIONS:

1. Toss shrimp with honey, soy sauce, garlic, lemon juice, gochujang, and oil until well coated. Cover and set aside for 30 minutes.
2. Preheat the air fryer to 350 F/ 176 C.
3. Thread shrimp onto the soaked skewers.
4. Place shrimp skewers onto an airflow rack lined with parchment paper on the middle shelf of the air fryer and cook for 8 minutes.
5. Serve and enjoy.

Healthy Crab Patties

PER SERVING:
CALORIES 153, CARBS 4.4G, FAT 10.2G, PROTEIN 9.7G

COOK TIME: 10 MINUTES
SERVES: 4
INGREDIENTS:

- Crab meat - 8 oz
- Egg, lightly beaten - 1
- Old bay seasoning - 1/2 tsp
- Green onion, sliced - 1
- Butter, melted - 2 tbsp
- Dijon mustard - 2 tsp
- Mayonnaise - 1 tbsp
- Parsley, chopped - 2 tbsp
- Almond flour - 1/4 cup
- Pepper
- Salt

DIRECTIONS:

1. Preheat the air fryer to 350 F/ 176 C.
2. Add crab meat and remaining ingredients in a mixing bowl until well combined.
3. Make patties from the meat mixture and place them onto an airflow rack lined with parchment paper on the middle shelf of the air fryer and cook for 10 minutes.
4. Serve and enjoy.

Lemon Pepper Tuna Steak

PER SERVING:
CALORIES 310, CARBS 3.5G, FAT 15.2G, PROTEIN 38.1G

COOK TIME: 20 MINUTES
SERVES: 2
INGREDIENTS:

- Tuna steaks - 8 oz
- Onion powder - 1/8 tsp
- Parmesan cheese, grated - 1 tbsp
- Almond flour - 1 tbsp
- Lemon pepper seasoning - 1/8 tsp
- Italian seasoning - 1/4 tsp
- Garlic powder - 1/8 tsp
- Pepper
- Salt

DIRECTIONS:

1. Preheat the air fryer to 375 F/ 190 C.
2. Mix almond flour, garlic powder, Italian seasoning, cheese, onion powder, lemon pepper seasoning, pepper, and salt in a shallow dish.
3. Coat tuna steaks with almond flour mixture.
4. Place tuna steaks onto an airflow rack lined with parchment paper on the middle shelf of the air fryer and cook for 20 minutes.
5. Serve and enjoy.

POULTRY RECIPES

Healthy Chicken Fajitas

PER SERVING:
CALORIES 202, CARBS 9G, FAT 6G, PROTEIN 25G

COOK TIME: 17 MINUTES
SERVES: 4
INGREDIENTS:

- Chicken breast, boneless, skinless & cut into strips - 1 lb
- Olive oil - 1 tbsp
- Onion, cut into strips - 1 large
- Yellow bell pepper, cut into strips - 1
- Red bell pepper, cut into strips - 1
- Cayenne pepper - 1/4 tsp
- Garlic powder - 1/2 tsp
- Onion powder - 1/2 tsp
- Cumin - 1/2 tsp
- Smoked paprika - 1 tsp
- Chili powder - 2 tsp
- Salt - 3/4 tsp

DIRECTIONS:

1. Preheat the air fryer to 390 F/ 200 C.
2. In a small bowl, mix all seasoning ingredients and set aside.
3. Mix chicken, onion, bell peppers, and olive oil in a large mixing bowl, sprinkle seasoning over chicken mixture, and toss until well coated.
4. Spread chicken mixture onto an airflow rack lined with parchment paper on the middle shelf of the air fryer and cook for 15-17 minutes.
5. Serve and enjoy.

Perfect Lemon Pepper Chicken

PER SERVING:
CALORIES 283, CARBS 1.5G, FAT 15.4G, PROTEIN 33.1G

COOK TIME: 20 MINUTES
SERVES: 4
INGREDIENTS:

- Chicken breasts, boneless and skinless - 4
- Onion powder - 1/2 tsp
- Garlic powder - 1 tsp
- Lemon pepper seasoning - 1 tbsp
- Olive oil - 2 tbsp

DIRECTIONS:

1. Toss chicken with onion powder, garlic powder, lemon pepper seasoning, and olive oil until well coated in a large bowl.
2. Place chicken onto an airflow rack lined with parchment paper on the middle shelf of the air fryer.
3. Air fry chicken at 390 F/ 198 C for 20 minutes.
4. Serve and enjoy.

Juicy Honey Dijon Chicken

PER SERVING:
CALORIES 306, CARBS 14G, FAT 12G, PROTEIN 33G

COOK TIME: 12 MINUTES
SERVES: 4
INGREDIENTS:

- Chicken tenders - 1 lb
- Dried oregano - 2 tsp
- Honey - 3 tbsp
- Dijon mustard - 1/4 cup
- Olive oil - 1 tbsp
- Pepper
- Salt

DIRECTIONS:

1. In a large bowl, add chicken tenders and season with pepper and salt.
2. Add oregano, honey, Dijon mustard, and olive oil over chicken tenders and toss to coat.
3. Place chicken tenders onto an airflow rack lined with parchment paper on the middle shelf of the air fryer.
4. Air fry chicken tenders at 380 F/ 193 C for 12 minutes.
5. Serve and enjoy.

Juicy & Tender Chicken Bites

PER SERVING:
CALORIES 466, CARBS 1G, FAT 20.9G, PROTEIN 65G

COOK TIME: 12 MINUTES
SERVES: 4
INGREDIENTS:

- Chicken breasts, boneless, skinless & cut into 1 ½-inch pieces - 2 lbs
- Fresh parsley, minced - 3 tsp
- Red pepper flakes - 1/8 tsp
- Poultry seasoning - 1 tsp
- Lemon pepper - 1 ½ tsp
- Olive oil - 1 tbsp
- Garlic salt - 3/4 tsp

DIRECTIONS:

1. Preheat the air fryer to 380 F/ 193 C.
2. In a mixing bowl, toss chicken with red pepper flakes, poultry seasoning, lemon pepper, olive oil, and garlic salt until well coated.
3. Add chicken onto an airflow rack lined with parchment paper on the middle shelf of the air fryer and cook for 12 minutes.
4. Garnish with parsley and serve.

Blackened Chicken

PER SERVING:
CALORIES 247, CARBS 3G, FAT 10G, PROTEIN 33.5G

COOK TIME: 12 MINUTES
SERVES: 4
INGREDIENTS:

- Chicken tenders - 1 lb
- Red pepper flakes - 1/4 tsp
- Oregano - 1 tsp
- Cumin - 1 tsp
- Garlic powder - 2 tsp
- Paprika - 2 tsp
- Onion powder - 2 tsp
- Olive oil - 1/2 tbsp
- Pepper - 1 tsp
- Salt - 1 tsp

DIRECTIONS:

1. Preheat the air fryer to 390 F/ 198 C.
2. In a large mixing bowl, toss chicken tenders with olive oil. Add spices and toss chicken until well coated.
3. Add chicken tenders onto an airflow rack lined with parchment paper on the middle shelf of the air fryer and cook for 12 minutes.
4. Serve and enjoy.

Chicken & Broccoli

PER SERVING:
CALORIES 279, CARBS 6G, FAT 12.7G, PROTEIN 35.1G

COOK TIME: 10 MINUTES
SERVES: 4
INGREDIENTS:

- Chicken breasts, boneless, skinless & cut into 1 ½-inch pieces - 1 lb
- Dried basil - 1 tsp
- Lemon pepper seasoning - 2 tsp
- Olive oil - 1 tbsp
- Broccoli florets - 4 cups
- Salt - 1/4 tsp

DIRECTIONS:

1. In a mixing bowl, toss chicken with basil, lemon pepper seasoning, olive oil, broccoli florets, and salt until well coated.
2. Add chicken and broccoli mixture onto an airflow rack lined with parchment paper on the middle shelf of the air fryer and cook at 400 F/ 204 C for 10 minutes.
3. Serve and enjoy.

Flavorful Chicken Breasts

PER SERVING:
CALORIES 329, CARBS 1G, FAT 21G, PROTEIN 33G

COOK TIME: 10 MINUTES
SERVES: 4
INGREDIENTS:

- Chicken breasts, skinless & boneless - 4
- Lemon juice - 1 ½ tbsp
- Dried tarragon - 1 tsp
- Dried thyme - 1 tsp
- Dried parsley - 1 tsp
- Dried basil - 1 tsp
- Garlic powder - 1 tsp
- Onion powder - 1 tsp
- Olive oil - 1/4 cup
- Pepper
- Salt

DIRECTIONS:

1. Preheat the air fryer to 370 F/ 187 C.
2. Add chicken into the large mixing bowl, then add remaining ingredients and mix until chicken is well coated.
3. Place chicken onto an airflow rack lined with parchment paper on the middle shelf of the air fryer and cook for 10 minutes.
4. Slice and serve.

Classic Greek Chicken

PER SERVING:
CALORIES 283, CARBS 1.5G, FAT 10.8G, PROTEIN 42.3G

COOK TIME: 15 MINUTES
SERVES: 3
INGREDIENTS:

- Chicken breasts, skinless & boneless - 3
- Parsley - 1 tsp
- Fresh oregano - 1 tsp
- Fresh thyme - 1 tsp
- Garlic, minced - 1 tsp
- Lemon juice - 1 tbsp
- Pepper
- Salt

DIRECTIONS:

1. Add chicken and remaining ingredients into the mixing bowl and mix until well coated. Cover and place in refrigerator for overnight.
2. Place marinated chicken onto an airflow rack lined with parchment paper on the middle shelf of the air fryer and cook at 400 F/ 204 C for 12-15 minutes.
3. Slice and serve.

Crispy Chicken Wings

PER SERVING:
CALORIES 398, CARBS 4G, FAT 19.7G, PROTEIN 49.9G

COOK TIME: 10 MINUTES
SERVES: 4
INGREDIENTS:

- Chicken wings - 1 ½ lbs
- Baking powder - 1 tbsp
- Smoked paprika - 1 tsp
- Brown sugar - 1 tbsp
- Olive oil - 2 tbsp
- Pepper
- Salt

DIRECTIONS:

1. Preheat the air fryer to 375 F/ 190 C.
2. In a large bowl, toss chicken wings with baking powder, smoked paprika, brown sugar, olive oil, pepper, and salt until well coated.
3. Add chicken wings onto an airflow rack lined with parchment paper on the middle shelf of the air fryer and cook for 10 minutes.
4. Serve and enjoy.

Flavors Chicken Legs

PER SERVING:
CALORIES 313, CARBS 1.7G, FAT 14G, PROTEIN 42.2G

COOK TIME: 20 MINUTES
SERVES: 8
INGREDIENTS:

- Chicken legs - 8
- Brown sugar - 2 tsp
- Smoked paprika - 2 tsp
- Olive oil - 2 tbsp
- Garlic powder - 1/2 tsp
- Pepper - 1/4 tsp
- Salt - 1 tsp

DIRECTIONS:

1. Preheat the air fryer to 400 F/ 204 C.
2. Add chicken legs, paprika, pepper, oil, garlic powder, brown sugar, and salt into the mixing bowl and toss until well coated.
3. Arrange chicken legs onto an airflow rack lined with parchment paper on the middle shelf of the air fryer and cook for 20 minutes.
4. Serve and enjoy.

Healthy Turkey Patties

PER SERVING:
CALORIES 235, CARBS 1.5G, FAT 12G, PROTEIN 32G

COOK TIME: 14 MINUTES
SERVES: 4
INGREDIENTS:

- Egg white - 1
- Ground turkey - 1 lb
- Worcestershire sauce - 2 tbsp
- Paprika - 1/4 tsp
- Dried basil - 1/2 tsp
- Dried oregano - 1/2 tsp
- Pepper
- Salt

DIRECTIONS:

1. Preheat the air fryer to 360 F/ 182 C.
2. Add all ingredients into the bowl and mix until well combined.
3. Make equal shapes of balls from the meat mixture and place them onto an air flow rack lined with parchment paper on the middle shelf of the air fryer.
4. Cook meatballs on air fry mode for 14 minutes.
5. Serve and enjoy.

Cheese Bacon Chicken

PER SERVING:
CALORIES 565, CARBS 1.5G, FAT 38G, PROTEIN 52G

COOK TIME: 30 MINUTES
SERVES: 4
INGREDIENTS:

- Chicken breasts, boneless & skinless - 4
- Cream cheese - 6 oz
- Olive oil - 1 tbsp
- Cheddar cheese, shredded - 1 cup
- Bacon slices, cooked & chopped - 8
- Pepper
- Salt

DIRECTIONS:

1. Preheat the air fryer to 400 F/ 204 C.
2. Spray the casserole dish with cooking spray.
3. Season chicken breasts with pepper and salt and place in casserole dish.
4. Add cream cheese, bacon, and cheddar cheese on top of the chicken breasts, then place the casserole dish on the bottom shelf of the air fryer.
5. Bake chicken for 28-30 minutes.
6. Serve and enjoy.

Tasty Chicken Meatballs

PER SERVING:
CALORIES 215, CARBS 11G, FAT 7G, PROTEIN 24G

COOK TIME: 20 MINUTES
SERVES: 6
INGREDIENTS:

- Egg - 1
- Ground chicken - 1 lb
- Cilantro, minced - 1 tbsp
- Breadcrumbs - 1/2 cup
- Lime zest - 1/2
- Green onion, minced - 2 tbsp
- Sweet chili sauce - 1/4 cup
- Garlic, grated - 2 tsp
- Lemongrass, grated - 1 tbsp
- Ginger, grated - 1 tbsp
- Pepper
- Salt

DIRECTIONS:

1. Preheat the air fryer to 350 F/ 176 C.
2. Add all ingredients except chili sauce into the mixing bowl and mix until well combined.
3. Make equal shapes of balls from the meat mixture and place them onto an airflow rack lined with parchment paper on the middle shelf of the air fryer.
4. Bake meatballs for 10 minutes.
5. After 10 minutes, brush meatballs with chili sauce and bake for 10 more.
6. Serve and enjoy.

Crispy Chicken

PER SERVING:
CALORIES 395, CARBS 17G, FAT 13G, PROTEIN 47G

COOK TIME: 30 MINUTES
SERVES: 4
INGREDIENTS:

- Egg - 1
- Chicken thighs, boneless & skinless - 20 oz
- Balsamic vinegar - 1 tbsp
- All-purpose flour - 2 tbsp
- Fresh basil, chopped - 2 tbsp
- Parmesan cheese, grated - 1/4 cup
- Breadcrumbs - 3/4 cup
- Pepper
- Salt

DIRECTIONS:

1. In a shallow dish, add flour.
2. In a separate shallow dish, whisk the egg with vinegar and salt.
3. In a third shallow dish, mix breadcrumbs and cheese.
4. Coat chicken with flour, dip into the egg mixture, and then coat with breadcrumbs.
5. Place coated chicken onto an air flow rack lined with parchment paper on the middle shelf of the air fryer.
6. Cook chicken on air fry mode at 325 F/ 162 C for 30 minutes.
7. Serve and enjoy.

Easy & Juicy Chicken Wings

PER SERVING:
CALORIES 550, CARBS 1G, FAT 29G, PROTEIN 65G

COOK TIME: 30 MINUTES
SERVES: 2
INGREDIENTS:

- Chicken wings - 1 lb
- Sriracha sauce - 2 tbsp
- Olive oil - 1 tsp
- Garlic powder - 1/4 tsp
- Onion powder - 1/4 tsp
- Pepper
- Salt

DIRECTIONS:

1. Toss chicken wings with oil, garlic powder, onion powder, sriracha sauce, salt, and pepper in a mixing bowl until well coated.
2. Arrange chicken wings onto an airflow rack lined with parchment paper on the middle shelf of the air fryer.
3. Cook chicken wings on air fry mode at 400 F/ 204 C for 30 minutes.
4. Serve and enjoy.

Honey Sriracha Chicken Wings

PER SERVING:
CALORIES 310, CARBS 18G, FAT 11G, PROTEIN 33G

COOK TIME: 30 MINUTES
SERVES: 4
INGREDIENTS:

- Chicken wings - 1 lb
- Soy sauce - 1 1/2 tbsp
- Sriracha sauce - 2 tbsp
- Lime juice - 1/2
- Butter, melted - 1 tbsp
- Honey - 1/4 cup
- Pepper
- Salt

DIRECTIONS:

1. Preheat the air fryer to 360 F/ 182 C.
2. Season chicken wings with pepper and salt.
3. Arrange chicken wings onto an airflow rack lined with parchment paper on the middle shelf of the air fryer.
4. Cook chicken wings on air fry mode for 30 minutes.
5. Add honey, butter, sriracha sauce, soy sauce, and lime juice in a small saucepan and mix well. Cook sauce for 3 minutes.
6. In a mixing bowl, toss chicken wings with sauce until well coated.
7. Serve and enjoy.

Flavorful Chicken Drumsticks

PER SERVING:
CALORIES 220, CARBS 1.2G, FAT 9G, PROTEIN 31.9G

COOK TIME: 25 MINUTES
SERVES: 6
INGREDIENTS:

- Chicken drumsticks - 1 1/2 lbs
- Ground cumin - 1/4 tsp
- Dried oregano - 1/2 tsp
- Cayenne - 1/4 tsp
- Paprika - 1 tsp
- Onion powder - 1/4 tsp
- Honey mustard sauce - 1 tsp
- Garlic powder - 1/2 tsp
- Butter, melted - 1 tbsp
- Olive oil - 1 tsp
- Dried parsley - 1 tsp
- Pepper
- Salt

DIRECTIONS:

1. Toss chicken drumsticks with the remaining ingredients in a mixing bowl until well coated.
2. Place chicken drumsticks onto an airflow rack lined with parchment paper on the middle shelf of the air fryer.
3. Cook chicken drumsticks on air fry mode at 375 F/ 190 C for 25 minutes.
4. Serve and enjoy.

Chicken Sausage with Veggies

PER SERVING:
CALORIES 147, CARBS 11G, FAT 8G, PROTEIN 8.4G

COOK TIME: 25 MINUTES
SERVES: 4
INGREDIENTS:

- Chicken sausage, sliced - 4
- Bell peppers, diced - 2
- Cherry tomatoes - 8 oz
- Cajun seasoning - 2 tsp
- Olive oil - 1 tbsp
- Mushrooms, sliced - 8 oz
- Pepper
- Salt

DIRECTIONS:

1. Add sausage slices onto an air flow rack lined with parchment paper on the middle shelf of the air fryer and air fry at 400 F/ 200 C for 8 minutes.
2. Toss bell peppers, mushrooms, tomatoes, oil, Cajun seasoning, pepper, and salt in a bowl.
3. Add vegetables, mushrooms, and tomatoes onto an airflow rack with sausage and cook for 20 minutes.
4. Stir well and serve.

Crispy Chicken Breast

PER SERVING:
CALORIES 320, CARBS 39G, FAT 5G, PROTEIN 26.3G

COOK TIME: 22 MINUTES
SERVES: 4
INGREDIENTS:

- Chicken breast, boneless & halves - 4
- Dijon mustard - 3/4 cup
- Maple syrup - 1/3 cup
- Breadcrumbs - 1 cup
- Pepper
- Salt

DIRECTIONS:

1. In a shallow dish, mix breadcrumbs, pepper, and salt.
2. In a separate shallow dish, mix maple syrup and Dijon mustard.
3. Dip each chicken breast in maple syrup mixture and coat with breadcrumbs.
4. Place coated chicken onto an airflow rack lined with parchment paper on the middle shelf of the air fryer.
5. Cook on air fry mode at 325 F/ 162 C for 22 minutes.
6. Serve and enjoy.

Chicken Casserole

PER SERVING:
CALORIES 605, CARBS 12G, FAT 42.4G, PROTEIN 42.2G

COOK TIME: 15 MINUTES
SERVES: 4
INGREDIENTS:

- Chicken, cooked & diced - 2 cups
- Heavy cream - 1 tbsp
- Half & half - 2 cups
- Swiss cheese slices - 8
- Nutmeg - 1/2 tsp
- Chips, crushed - 1 oz
- Dijon mustard - 2 tsp
- Butter, melted - 2 tbsp
- Ham, diced - 1/2 cup

DIRECTIONS:

1. Add ham and chicken into the greased baking pan and mix well. Top with cheese slices.
2. In a bowl, mix half & half butter, nutmeg, heavy cream, and Dijon mustard, and pour over chicken. Sprinkle crushed chips on top.
3. Place the baking pan on the bottom shelf of the air fryer and cook at 350 F/ 176 C for 15 minutes.
4. Serve and enjoy.

MEAT RECIPES

Classic Steak Bites

PER SERVING:
CALORIES 294, CARBS 0.9G, FAT 10.2G, PROTEIN 46.9G

COOK TIME: 12 MINUTES
SERVES: 4
INGREDIENTS:

- Sirloin steak, cut into 1 ½-inch pieces - 2 lbs
- Soy sauce, low-sodium - 1 ½ tsp
- Olive oil - 2 tbsp
- Pepper - 1 ½ tsp
- Salt - 1 ½ tsp

DIRECTIONS:

1. Preheat the air fryer to 400 F/ 204 C.
2. Toss steak chunks with soy sauce, olive oil, pepper, and salt in a mixing bowl until well coated.
3. Spread steak chunks onto an airflow rack lined with parchment paper on the middle shelf of the air fryer and cook for 12 minutes.
4. Serve and enjoy.

Lamb Patties

PER SERVING:
CALORIES 220, CARBS 2G, FAT 8G, PROTEIN 32G

COOK TIME: 15 MINUTES
SERVES: 4
INGREDIENTS:

- Ground lamb - 1 lb
- Garlic, minced - 1 tbsp
- Ground coriander - 1 tsp
- Ground cumin - 1 tsp
- Fresh parsley, chopped - 1/4 cup
- Onion, minced - 1/4 cup
- Cayenne pepper - 1/4 tsp
- Ground cinnamon - 1 tsp
- Pepper
- Salt

DIRECTIONS:

1. Preheat the air fryer to 400 F/ 204 C.
2. Add all ingredients into the bowl and mix until well combined.
3. Make equal shapes of patties from the meat mixture and place them onto an airflow rack lined with parchment paper on the middle shelf of the air fryer.
4. Bake patties for 15 minutes.
5. Serve and enjoy.

Lamb Meatballs

PER SERVING:
CALORIES 325, CARBS 1G, FAT 20G, PROTEIN 3G

COOK TIME: 20 MINUTES
SERVES: 4
INGREDIENTS:

- Egg, lightly beaten - 1
- Ground lamb - 1 lb
- Fresh parsley, chopped - 2 tbsp
- Garlic, minced - 1 tbsp
- Ground cumin - 1 tsp
- Olive oil - 3 tbsp
- Red pepper flakes - 1/4 tsp
- Fresh oregano, chopped - 2 tsp
- Pepper
- Salt

DIRECTIONS:

1. Preheat the air fryer to 400 F/ 204 C.
2. Add all ingredients into the bowl and mix until well combined.
3. Make equal shapes of balls from the meat mixture and place them onto an airflow rack lined with parchment paper on the middle shelf of the air fryer.
4. Bake meatballs for 20 minutes.
5. Serve and enjoy.

Beef Meatballs

PER SERVING:
CALORIES 300, CARBS 2G, FAT 10G, PROTEIN 47G

COOK TIME: 20 MINUTES
SERVES: 6
INGREDIENTS:

- Egg, lightly beaten - 1
- Ground beef - 2 lbs
- Smoked paprika - 1 tsp
- Oregano - 1 tsp
- Cinnamon - 1 tsp
- Cumin - 2 tsp
- Coriander - 2 tsp
- Fresh mint, chopped - 1 tbsp
- Fresh cilantro, minced - 1/4 cup
- Garlic, minced - 1 tsp
- Small onion, grated - 1
- Pepper
- Salt

DIRECTIONS:

1. Preheat the air fryer to 400 F/ 204 C.
2. Add all ingredients into the bowl and mix until well combined.
3. Make equal shapes of balls from the meat mixture and place them onto an airflow rack lined with parchment paper on the middle shelf of the air fryer.
4. Bake meatballs for 20 minutes.
5. Serve and enjoy.

Meatloaf

PER SERVING:
CALORIES 320, CARBS 3.9G, FAT 11G, PROTEIN 48G

COOK TIME: 50 MINUTES
SERVES: 6
INGREDIENTS:

- Eggs, lightly beaten - 2
- Ground beef - 2 lbs
- Paprika - 1 tsp
- Cumin - 1 tsp
- Green onion, chopped - 1/4 cup
- Oregano - 1 tsp
- Salsa - 1/2 cup
- Fresh cilantro, chopped - 1/4 cup
- Red bell pepper diced and sautéed - 1
- Sunflower seed flour - 1/2 cup
- Salt - 1/2 tsp

DIRECTIONS:

1. Preheat the air fryer to 375 F/ 190 C.
2. Spray a loaf pan with cooking spray and set aside.
3. Add all ingredients into the bowl and mix until well combined.
4. Transfer the meat mixture to the loaf pan and place the pan on the bottom shelf of the air fryer.
5. Bake meatloaf for 50 minutes.
6. Slice and serve.

Ranch Garlic Pork Chops

PER SERVING:
CALORIES 328, CARBS 0.2G, FAT 28G, PROTEIN 18G

COOK TIME: 30 MINUTES
SERVES: 6
INGREDIENTS:

- Pork chops, boneless - 6
- Garlic, minced - 1 tsp
- Ranch seasoning - 2 tbsp
- Olive oil - 1/4 cup
- Dried parsley - 1 tsp
- Pepper
- Salt

DIRECTIONS:

1. Preheat the air fryer to 400 F/ 204 C.
2. Season pork chops with pepper and salt and place into the baking dish.
3. Mix olive oil, parsley, garlic, and ranch seasoning and pour over pork chops.
4. Place the baking dish on the middle shelf of the air fryer and bake pork chops for 30 minutes.
5. Serve and enjoy.

Baked Herb Meatballs

PER SERVING:
CALORIES 304, CARBS 14G, FAT 9G, PROTEIN 38G

COOK TIME: 25 MINUTES
SERVES: 4
INGREDIENTS:

- Egg, lightly beaten - 1
- Ground beef - 1 pound
- Green onions, chopped - 2 small
- Lemon juice - 1
- Pepper - ½ tsp
- Breadcrumbs - 2/3 cup
- Garlic cloves, minced - 2
- Dried thyme - 2 tsp
- Salt - ½ tsp

DIRECTIONS:

1. Preheat the air fryer to 375 F/ 190 C.
2. Add ground beef and remaining ingredients into the mixing bowl and mix until well combined.
3. Make equal shapes of meatballs from the meat mixture and place an airflow rack lined with parchment paper on the middle shelf of the air fryer.
4. Bake meatballs for 25 minutes.
5. Serve and enjoy.

Meatloaf

PER SERVING:
CALORIES 289, CARBS 8G, FAT 9G, PROTEIN 37G

COOK TIME: 20 MINUTES
SERVES: 6
INGREDIENTS:

- Eggs, lightly beaten - 2
- Ground beef - 1 1/2 lbs
- Garlic clove, minced - 1
- Onion, grated - 1/2
- Bourbon - 2 tbsp
- Breadcrumbs - 1/2 cup
- Milk - 1/4 cup
- Steak seasoning - 1 tbsp
- Worcestershire sauce - 1 tbsp
- Pepper
- Salt

DIRECTIONS:

1. Preheat the air fryer to 350 F/ 176 C.
2. Add ground beef and remaining ingredients in a bowl and mix until well combined.
3. Transfer the meat mixture to the greased loaf pan.
4. Place the loaf pan on the bottom shelf of the air fryer and cook on air fry mode for 20 minutes.
5. Slice and serve.

Juicy Flank Steak

PER SERVING:
CALORIES 285, CARBS 1G, FAT 19.5G, PROTEIN 24.9G

COOK TIME: 10 MINUTES
SERVES: 4
INGREDIENTS:

- Flank steak - 4
- Worcestershire sauce - 1 tbsp
- Soy sauce - 1 tbsp
- Red wine vinegar - 1/4 cup
- Garlic, minced - 1 tsp
- Dijon mustard - 1 tbsp
- Olive oil - 1/4 cup
- Pepper
- Salt

DIRECTIONS:

1. Mix flank steak with oil, soy sauce, vinegar, pepper, garlic, mustard, Worcestershire sauce, and salt in a large bowl. Cover and set aside to marinate for 30 minutes.
2. Preheat the air fryer to 350 F/ 176 C.
3. Place marinated steak onto an air flow rack lined with parchment paper on the middle shelf of the air fryer.
4. Cook steak on air fry mode for 10 minutes.
5. Serve and enjoy.

Marinated Pork Chops

PER SERVING:
CALORIES 305, CARBS 13G, FAT 19G, PROTEIN 18G

COOK TIME: 12 MINUTES
SERVES: 2
INGREDIENTS:

- Pork chops, boneless - 2
- Water - 1 tbsp
- Rice wine - 1 tbsp
- Dark soy sauce - 1 tbsp
- Light soy sauce - 1 tbsp
- Cinnamon - 1/2 tsp
- Five-spice powder - 1/2 tsp
- Black pepper - 1 tsp
- Sugar - 1 1/2 tbsp

DIRECTIONS:

1. Add pork chops and remaining ingredients into the zip-lock bag. Seal the bag and place it in the refrigerator for 4 hours.
2. Place marinated pork chops onto an airflow rack lined with parchment paper on the middle shelf of the air fryer.
3. Cook pork chops on air fry mode at 380 F/ 193 C for 12 minutes.
4. Serve and enjoy.

Chili Lime Flank Steak

PER SERVING:
CALORIES 240, CARBS 1.5G, FAT 11G, PROTEIN 32G

COOK TIME: 10 MINUTES
SERVES: 4
INGREDIENTS:

- Flank steak, sliced - 1 lb
- Chili powder - 2 tsp
- Cumin - 1 tsp
- Olive oil - 1 tsp
- Soy sauce, low-sodium - 4 tsp
- Cilantro, chopped - 1/3 cup
- Cayenne - 1/4 tsp
- Lime juice - 3 tbsp
- Salt - 1/4 tsp

DIRECTIONS:

1. Add steak pieces and remaining ingredients into the zip-lock bag. Seal the bag and place it in the refrigerator for 4 hours.
2. Place marinated meat onto an airflow rack lined with parchment paper on the middle shelf of the air fryer.
3. Cook on air fry mode at 380 F/ 193 C for 10 minutes.
4. Serve and enjoy.

Easy Pork Skewers

PER SERVING:
CALORIES 518, CARBS 12G, FAT 34G, PROTEIN 38G

COOK TIME: 10 MINUTES
SERVES: 3
INGREDIENTS:

- Pork shoulder, cut into 1/4-inch pieces - 1 lb
- Soy sauce - 4 1/2 tbsp
- Garlic, crushed - 1/2 tbsp
- Ginger paste - 1 tbsp
- Sesame oil - 1 1/2 tsp
- Rice vinegar - 1 1/2 tbsp
- Honey - 1 1/2 tbsp
- Pepper
- Salt

DIRECTIONS:

1. In a mixing bowl, mix meat with the remaining ingredients. Cover and place in refrigerator for 60 minutes.
2. Preheat the air fryer to 350 F/ 176 C.
3. Thread marinated meat onto the soaked skewers.
4. Place meat skewers onto an airflow rack lined with parchment paper on the middle shelf of the air fryer.
5. Cook on air fry mode for 10 minutes.
6. Serve and enjoy.

Flavorful Honey Pork Chops

PER SERVING:
CALORIES 495, CARBS 23G, FAT 33G, PROTEIN 25.4G

COOK TIME: 12 MINUTES
SERVES: 4
INGREDIENTS:

- Pork chops, boneless - 1 lb
- Brown mustard - 1/4 cup
- Mayonnaise - 1/4 cup
- BBQ sauce - 2 tbsp
- Honey - 1/4 cup
- Pepper
- Salt

DIRECTIONS:

1. In a mixing bowl, coat pork chops with mustard, honey, mayonnaise, BBQ sauce, pepper, and salt. Cover bowl and place in refrigerator for 1 hour.
2. Place marinated pork chops onto an air flow rack lined with parchment paper on the middle shelf of the air fryer.
3. Cook pork chops on air fry mode at 360 F/ 182 C for 12 minutes.
4. Serve and enjoy.

Lemon Pepper Pork Tenderloin

PER SERVING:
CALORIES 275, CARBS 3G, FAT 7G, PROTEIN 45G

COOK TIME: 20 MINUTES
SERVES: 4
INGREDIENTS:

- Pork tenderloin - 1 1/2 lbs
- Lemon pepper seasoning - 1 tsp
- Brown sugar - 1 tbsp
- Onion powder - 1 tsp
- Olive oil - 1 1/2 tsp
- Smoked paprika - 1 tsp
- Pepper
- Salt

DIRECTIONS:

1. Preheat the air fryer to 400 F/ 204 C.
2. Mix onion powder, paprika, brown sugar, lemon pepper seasoning, pepper, and salt in a small bowl.
3. Brush pork tenderloin with oil and rub with spice mixture.
4. Place pork tenderloin onto an airflow rack lined with parchment paper on the middle shelf of the air fryer.
5. Cook pork tenderloin on air fry mode for 20 minutes.
6. Slice and serve.

Balsamic Pork Tenderloin

PER SERVING:
CALORIES 230, CARBS 5G, FAT 5G, PROTEIN 37.7G

COOK TIME: 20 MINUTES
SERVES: 4
INGREDIENTS:

- Pork tenderloin - 1 1/4 lbs
- Brown sugar - 2 tbsp
- Lemon juice - 1 tbsp
- Soy sauce - 2 tbsp
- Balsamic vinegar - 3 tbsp
- Garlic powder - 1/2 tsp
- Onion powder - 1/2 tsp
- Dried rosemary, crushed - 1 tsp
- Pepper
- Salt

DIRECTIONS:

1. Coat pork tenderloin with brown sugar, rosemary, onion powder, vinegar, soy sauce, lemon juice, garlic powder, pepper, and salt in a bowl. Cover and place in refrigerator for overnight.
2. Preheat the air fryer to 400 F/ 204 C.
3. Place marinated pork tenderloin onto an airflow rack lined with parchment paper on the middle shelf of the air fryer and cook for 20 minutes.
4. Slice and serve.

Juicy & Tender Pork Loin

PER SERVING:
CALORIES 285, CARBS 3G, FAT 15G, PROTEIN 31G

COOK TIME: 18 MINUTES
SERVES: 8
INGREDIENTS:

- Pork loin - 2 lbs
- Garlic powder - 1 tsp
- Brown sugar - 3 tbsp
- Onion powder - 1/4 tsp
- Paprika - 1/4 tsp
- Basil - 1 tsp
- Pepper
- Salt

DIRECTIONS:

1. Preheat the air fryer to 400 F/ 204 C.
2. Mix brown sugar, onion powder, paprika, basil, garlic powder, pepper, and salt in a small bowl and rub over pork loin.
3. Place pork loin onto an airflow rack lined with parchment paper on the middle shelf of the air fryer.
4. Cook on air fry mode for 18 minutes.
5. Slice and serve.

Pork Bites with Mushrooms

PER SERVING:
CALORIES 425, CARBS 2G, FAT 34.1G, PROTEIN 27.5G

COOK TIME: 15 MINUTES
SERVES: 4
INGREDIENTS:

- Pork chops, cut into 1-inch pieces - 1 lb
- Butter, melted - 2 tbsp
- Mushrooms, halved - 8 oz
- Garlic powder - 1/2 tsp
- Soy sauce - 1 tsp
- Pepper
- Salt

DIRECTIONS:

1. Preheat the air fryer to 400 F/ 204 C.
2. Mix pork chop pieces with butter, mushrooms, garlic powder, soy sauce, pepper, and salt in a mixing bowl.
3. Add pork and mushroom mixture onto an airflow rack lined with parchment paper on the middle shelf of the air fryer.
4. Cook on air fry mode for 15 minutes.
5. Serve and enjoy.

Parmesan Pork Chops

PER SERVING:
CALORIES 364, CARBS 2G, FAT 29.4G, PROTEIN 22.7G

COOK TIME: 12 MINUTES
SERVES: 4
INGREDIENTS:

- Pork chops - 4
- Garlic powder - 2 tsp
- Smoked paprika - 1 tsp
- Parmesan cheese, grated - 1/2 cup
- Olive oil - 2 tbsp
- Dried herbs - 1/2 tsp
- Ground mustard - 1 tsp
- Onion powder - 1 tsp
- Pepper
- Salt

DIRECTIONS:

1. Mix parmesan cheese, mustard, dried herbs, paprika, garlic powder, onion powder, pepper, and salt in a shallow dish.
2. Brush pork chops with oil and coat with cheese mixture.
3. Place coated pork chops onto an airflow rack lined with parchment paper on the middle shelf of the air fryer.
4. Cook pork chops on air fry mode at 400 F/ 204 C for 12 minutes.
5. Serve and enjoy.

Spicy Steak Bites

PER SERVING:
CALORIES 295, CARBS 2.4G, FAT 12.8G, PROTEIN 43G

COOK TIME: 10 MINUTES
SERVES: 4
INGREDIENTS:

- Sirloin steak cut into 1-inch pieces - 1 1/4 lbs
- Jalapeno pepper, minced - 1/2
- Garlic clove, minced - 1
- Butter, melted - 1 tbsp
- Lime juice - 1
- Lime zest, grated - 1
- Chili powder - 2 tsp
- Pepper
- Salt

DIRECTIONS:

1. Toss steak pieces with the remaining ingredients in a mixing bowl until well coated.
2. Add steak pieces onto an airflow rack lined with parchment paper on the middle shelf of the air fryer.
3. Cook on air fry mode at 400 F/ 204 C for 10 minutes.
4. Serve and enjoy.

Flavorful Pork Cutlets

PER SERVING:
CALORIES 390, CARBS 34G, FAT 22G, PROTEIN 13G

COOK TIME: 12 MINUTES
SERVES: 4
INGREDIENTS:

- Pork cutlets - 4
- Honey - 2 tsp
- Olive oil - 1 tsp
- Thyme - 2 tsp
- Ground paprika - 1/2 tsp
- Dijon mustard - 1 tsp

DIRECTIONS:

1. Mix honey, paprika, oil, mustard, and thyme in a small bowl.
2. Brush pork cutlets with honey mixture and place them onto an airflow rack lined with parchment paper on the middle shelf of the air fryer.
3. Cook on air fry mode at 400 F/ 204 C for 12 minutes.
4. Serve and enjoy.

VEGETABLE RECIPES

Perfect Crispy Potatoes

PER SERVING:
CALORIES 75, CARBS 12G, FAT 2G, PROTEIN 1.5G

COOK TIME: 15 MINUTES
SERVES: 6
INGREDIENTS:

- Potatoes, cut into small chunks - 1 lb
- Oregano - 1 tsp
- Greek seasoning - 1 tsp
- Lemon zest, grated - 1 tsp
- Lemon juice - 1 tsp
- Olive oil - 1 tbsp
- Pepper
- Salt

DIRECTIONS:

1. In a mixing bowl, toss potatoes with oregano, Greek seasoning, lemon zest, lemon juice, olive oil, pepper, and salt until well coated.
2. Spread potatoes onto an airflow rack lined with parchment paper on the middle shelf of the air fryer.
3. Air fry potatoes at 400 F/ 200 C for 15 minutes.
4. Serve and enjoy.

Baked Mixed Vegetables

PER SERVING:
CALORIES 81, CARBS 10G, FAT 4G, PROTEIN 3G

COOK TIME: 13 MINUTES
SERVES: 4
INGREDIENTS:

- Zucchini, sliced & quartered - 1
- Broccoli florets - 1 cup
- Yellow squash, sliced & quartered - 1
- Balsamic vinegar - 1 tbsp
- Mushrooms, sliced - 3 oz
- Olive oil - 1 tbsp
- Bell pepper, chopped - 1
- Onion, chopped - 1
- Thyme - ¾ tsp
- Pepper
- Salt

DIRECTIONS:

1. Preheat the air fryer to 400 F/ 204 C.
2. Add zucchini, broccoli florets, bell pepper, onion, squash, mushrooms, and remaining ingredients in a mixing bowl and toss until well coated.
3. Spread vegetables onto an airflow rack lined with parchment paper on the middle shelf of the air fryer and bake for 13 minutes.
4. Serve and enjoy.

Zucchini Cheese Balls

PER SERVING:
CALORIES 59, CARBS 7G, FAT 1.5G, PROTEIN 3G

COOK TIME: 18 MINUTES
SERVES: 4
INGREDIENTS:

- Egg - 1
- Zucchini, shredded & squeezed - 1 cup
- Dried oregano - ½ tsp
- Parmesan cheese, grated - ¼ cup
- Breadcrumbs - 1/3 cup
- Garlic, grated - ½ tsp
- Dried basil - ½ tsp
- Parsley, chopped - 1 tbsp
- Fresh chives, chopped - 2 tbsp
- Pepper
- Salt

DIRECTIONS:

1. Preheat the air fryer to 400 F/ 204 C.
2. Add zucchini and remaining ingredients into the mixing bowl and mix until well combined.
3. Make equal shapes of balls from the zucchini mixture.
4. Place zucchini balls onto an airflow rack lined with parchment paper on the middle shelf of the air fryer and bake for 18 minutes.
5. Serve and enjoy.

Healthy Air Fried Mushrooms

PER SERVING:
CALORIES 148, CARBS 4G, FAT 14G, PROTEIN 3G

COOK TIME: 10 MINUTES
SERVES: 2
INGREDIENTS:

- Mushrooms, clean & sliced - 8 oz
- Soy sauce, low-sodium - 1 tsp
- Garlic powder - 1/2 tsp
- Olive oil - 2 tbsp
- Parsley, chopped - 1 tbsp
- Pepper
- Salt

DIRECTIONS:

1. Preheat the air fryer to 380 F/ 193 C.
2. Toss mushrooms with soy sauce, garlic powder, oil, parsley, pepper, and salt in a mixing bowl.
3. Spread mushrooms onto an airflow rack lined with parchment paper on the middle shelf of the air fryer and cook for 10 minutes.
4. Serve and enjoy.

Spinach Quinoa Patties

PER SERVING:
CALORIES 184, CARBS 31G, FAT 3G, PROTEIN 7G

COOK TIME: 13 MINUTES
SERVES: 4
INGREDIENTS:

- Egg - 1
- Spinach, chopped - 1 cup
- Quinoa, cooked - 2 cups
- Onion, chopped - 1/2 cup
- Carrot, peel & shredded - 1/2 cup
- Garlic, minced - 1 tsp
- Parsley, minced - 2 tbsp
- Breadcrumbs - 1 cup
- Parmesan cheese, grated - 1/4 cup
- Milk - 1/4 cup
- Pepper
- Salt

DIRECTIONS:

1. Add quinoa and remaining ingredients in a large bowl and mix until well combined.
2. Preheat the air fryer to 380 F/ 193 C.
3. Make equal shapes of patties from the quinoa mixture and place them onto an airflow rack lined with parchment paper on the middle shelf of the air fryer.
4. Cook patties on air fry mode for 10 minutes.
5. Serve and enjoy.

Mushroom & Green Beans

PER SERVING:
CALORIES 80, CARBS 7G, FAT 5G, PROTEIN 2G

COOK TIME: 20 MINUTES
SERVES: 6
INGREDIENTS:

- Green beans, cut into 2-inch pieces - 1 lb
- Onion, sliced - 1 small
- Mushrooms, sliced - 1/2 lb
- Italian seasoning - 1 tsp
- Olive oil - 2 tbsp
- Pepper
- Salt

DIRECTIONS:

1. Preheat the air fryer to 375 F/ 190 C.
2. In a bowl, toss green beans with the remaining ingredients.
3. Spread the green beans mixture onto an airflow rack lined with parchment paper on the middle shelf of the air fryer and cook for 20 minutes.
4. Serve and enjoy.

Herb Cauliflower

PER SERVING:
CALORIES 165, CARBS 9G, FAT 14G, PROTEIN 3G

COOK TIME: 10 MINUTES
SERVES: 4
INGREDIENTS:

- Cauliflower florets - 6 cups
- Lemon zest, grated - 1 tsp
- Thyme, minced - 1 tbsp
- Rosemary, minced - 1 tbsp
- Parsley, minced - 1/4 cup
- Red pepper flakes, crushed - 1/4 tsp
- Lemon juice - 2 tbsp
- Olive oil - 4 tbsp
- Salt - 1/2 tsp

DIRECTIONS:

1. Preheat the air fryer to 350 F/ 176 C.
2. Toss cauliflower florets with remaining ingredients in a mixing bowl until well coated.
3. Spread cauliflower florets onto an airflow rack lined with parchment paper on the middle shelf of the air fryer and cook for 10 minutes.
4. Serve and enjoy.

Balsamic Brussels Sprouts

PER SERVING:
CALORIES 50, CARBS 4G, FAT 2G, PROTEIN 1.5G

COOK TIME: 10 MINUTES
SERVES: 4
INGREDIENTS:

- Brussels sprouts, cut in half - 2 cups
- Olive oil - 1 tbsp
- Balsamic vinegar - 1 tbsp
- Garlic powder - 1/4 tsp
- Paprika - 1/4 tsp
- Onions, sliced - 1/2 cup
- Pepper
- Salt

DIRECTIONS:

1. Add Brussels sprouts, onion, garlic powder, paprika, vinegar, oil, pepper, and salt into the bowl and toss well.
2. Spread the Brussels sprouts mixture onto an airflow rack lined with parchment paper on the middle shelf of the air fryer.
3. Cook Brussels sprouts on air fry mode at 350 F/ 176 C for 10 minutes.
4. Serve and enjoy.

Crispy Potatoes & Green Beans

PER SERVING:
CALORIES 127, CARBS 22G, FAT 3.6G, PROTEIN 3.1G

COOK TIME: 25 MINUTES
SERVES: 4
INGREDIENTS:

- Potatoes, cut into pieces - 1 lb
- Olive oil - 1 tbsp
- Garlic powder - 1 tsp
- Green beans, trimmed - 8 oz
- Onion powder - 1/4 tsp
- Paprika - 1/4 tsp
- Pepper
- Salt

DIRECTIONS:

1. Preheat the air fryer to 390 F/ 198 C.
2. Toss green beans with potatoes, onion powder, paprika, oil, garlic powder, pepper, and salt in a bowl.
3. Spread the potatoes and green beans mixture onto an airflow rack lined with parchment paper on the middle shelf of the air fryer.
4. Cook on air fry mode for 25 minutes. Stir halfway through.
5. Serve and enjoy.

Delicious Cauliflower Patties

PER SERVING:
CALORIES 156, CARBS 11G, FAT 8G, PROTEIN 10G

COOK TIME: 8 MINUTES
SERVES: 4
INGREDIENTS:

- Eggs, lightly beaten - 2
- Cauliflower rice - 2 cups
- Dried basil - 1 tsp
- Parmesan cheese, grated - 1/4 cup
- Onion powder - 1/2 tsp
- Garlic powder - 1 tsp
- Breadcrumbs - 1/3 cup
- Mexican cheese, shredded - 1/2 cup
- Pepper
- Salt

DIRECTIONS:

1. Add cauliflower rice into the bowl and microwave for 5 minutes. Drain well.
2. Mix cauliflower rice and remaining ingredients in a mixing bowl until well combined.
3. Make equal shapes of patties from the cauliflower mixture and place them onto an airflow rack lined with parchment paper on the middle shelf of the air fryer.
4. Cook patties on air fry mode at 400 F/ 204 C for 8 minutes.
5. Serve and enjoy.

DESSERTS

Cinnamon Apple Slices

PER SERVING:
CALORIES 183, CARBS 28G, FAT 5G, PROTEIN 6.9G

COOK TIME: 30 MINUTES
SERVES: 4
INGREDIENTS:

- Apples, core & sliced - 4 medium
- Ground cinnamon - 1/4 tsp
- Butter, melted - 1 tbsp
- Ground nutmeg - 1/4 tsp

DIRECTIONS:

1. Preheat the air fryer to 375 F/ 190 C.
2. Add apple slices to the baking dish, drizzle with butter, and sprinkle with nutmeg and cinnamon.
3. Place the baking dish on the middle shelf of the air fryer and bake apple slices for 25-30 minutes.
4. Serve and enjoy.

Choco Chip Banana Muffins

PER SERVING:
CALORIES 90, CARBS 10G, FAT 5G, PROTEIN 6G

COOK TIME: 25 MINUTES
SERVES: 6
INGREDIENTS:

- Eggs - 3
- Egg whites - 1/2 cup
- Banana - 1
- Coconut oil, melted - 1 tbsp
- Coconut flour - 5 tbsp
- Chocolate chips - 1 1/2 tbsp
- Baking powder - 1 tsp

DIRECTIONS:

1. Preheat the air fryer to 350 F/ 176 C.
2. Spray the muffin pan with cooking spray and set aside.
3. In a mixing bowl, add banana and mash using a fork.
4. Add eggs, egg whites, and coconut oil and stir until well combined.
5. Add coconut flour, baking powder, and chocolate chips and stir until well combined.
6. Spoon batter into the prepared muffin pan and place the pan on the middle shelf of the air fryer.
7. Bake muffins for 20-25 minutes.
8. Serve and enjoy.

Lemon Loaf Cake

PER SERVING:
CALORIES 451, CARBS 63G, FAT 21G, PROTEIN 5G

COOK TIME: 55 MINUTES
SERVES: 8
INGREDIENTS:

- Eggs - 2
- Vanilla extract - 2 tsp
- All-purpose flour - 1 3/4 cups
- Granulated sugar - 1 cup
- Sour cream - 1 cup
- Lemon juice - 1/4 cup
- Lemon zest, grated - 1 tbsp
- Baking powder - 2 tsp
- Salt - 1/2 tsp
- Canola oil - 1/2 cup

DIRECTIONS:

1. Preheat the air fryer to 350 F/ 176 C.
2. Grease a 9*5-inch loaf pan with butter and set aside.
3. Mix flour, baking powder, and salt in a mixing bowl.
4. In a separate bowl, whisk together oil, lemon zest, eggs, sugar, sour cream, lemon juice, and vanilla until well combined.
5. Add flour mixture into the oil mixture and mix until well combined.
6. Pour batter into the prepared pan and place the pan on the bottom shelf of the air fryer.
7. Bake loaf cake for 45-55 minutes.
8. Remove from air fryer and allow to cool completely.
9. Slice and serve.

Sweet & Tangy Lemon Blondies

PER SERVING:
CALORIES 135, CARBS 19G, FAT 6G, PROTEIN 1.2G

COOK TIME: 25 MINUTES
SERVES: 16
INGREDIENTS:

- Egg - 1
- Egg yolk - 1
- Flour - 3/4 cup
- Lemon juice - 1/2 cup
- Lemon zest, grated - 1/2 lemon
- Sugar - 3/4 cup
- Salt - 1/4 tsp
- Butter, softened - 1 stick
- For Glaze:
- Lemon juice - 2 tbsp
- Powdered sugar - 3/4 cup

DIRECTIONS:

1. In a mixing bowl, beat butter and sugar until smooth and creamy.
2. Add egg, egg yolk, lemon zest, and lemon juice and mix until well combined.
3. Add flour and salt and mix until well combined.
4. Pour batter into a greased 8*8-inch baking pan and place the pan on the bottom shelf of the air fryer.
5. Bake blondies for 25 minutes at 350 F/ 176 C. Remove from air fryer and cool completely.
6. For glaze, mix powdered lemon juice and sugar and spread over blondies.
7. Slice and serve.

Chocolate Brownies

PER SERVING:
CALORIES 150, CARBS 21G, FAT 7G, PROTEIN 1.5G

COOK TIME: 20 MINUTES
SERVES: 16
INGREDIENTS:

- All-purpose flour - 1 1/3 cups
- Vegetable oil - 1/2 cup
- Water - 1/2 cup
- Sugar - 1 cup
- Baking powder - 1/2 tsp
- Cocoa powder - 1/3 cup
- Vanilla - 1/2 tsp
- Salt - 1/2 tsp

DIRECTIONS:

1. Preheat the air fryer to 350 F/ 176.
2. Mix flour, cocoa powder, sugar, baking powder, and salt in a large bowl.
3. In a small bowl, whisk oil, water, and vanilla.
4. Pour the oil mixture into the flour mixture and mix until well combined.
5. Pour batter into the greased baking pan and place the pan on the bottom shelf of the air fryer.
6. Bake brownies for 20 minutes.
7. Slice and serve.

Tasty Apple Pear Crisp

PER SERVING:
CALORIES 155, CARBS 27G, FAT 5G, PROTEIN 2G

COOK TIME: 30 MINUTES
SERVES: 4
INGREDIENTS:

- Quick oats - 6 tbsp
- Apple, core & diced - 1
- Butter, cut into pieces - 1 1/2 tbsp
- All-purpose flour - 3 tbsp
- Pumpkin pie spice - 1/2 tsp
- Lemon juice - 1 tsp
- Pear, core & diced - 1
- Brown sugar - 2 tbsp

DIRECTIONS:

1. Preheat the air fryer to 350 F/ 176 C.
2. Mix oats, brown sugar, pumpkin pie spice, and flour in a bowl. Add butter and mix well.
3. Mix apple, pear, and lemon juice in a baking pan and top with oat mixture.
4. Place a baking pan on the middle shelf of the air fryer and cook on air fry mode for 30 minutes.
5. Serve and enjoy.

Apple Berry Crumble

PER SERVING:
CALORIES 313, CARBS 51G, FAT 12G, PROTEIN 2G

COOK TIME: 15 MINUTES
SERVES: 2
INGREDIENTS:

- Apple, diced - 1
- Blueberries - 1/4 cup
- Strawberries, chopped - 1/4 cup
- Butter - 2 tbsp
- Cinnamon - 1/2 tsp
- Sugar - 2 tbsp
- Rice flour - 5 tbsp

DIRECTIONS:

1. Preheat the air fryer to 350 F/ 176 C.
2. Add apple, blueberries, and strawberries in a greased baking pan and mix well.
3. Mix rice flour, cinnamon, sugar, and butter in a small bowl and spread on top of the fruit mixture.
4. Place the baking pan on the middle shelf of the air fryer and cook on air fryer mode for 15 minutes.
5. Serve and enjoy.

Cinnamon Lemon Peaches

PER SERVING:
CALORIES 130, CARBS 19G, FAT 6G, PROTEIN 1.5G

COOK TIME: 07 MINUTES
SERVES: 4
INGREDIENTS:

- Ripe peaches, quartered & pitted - 4
- Brown sugar - 2 tbsp
- Butter, melted - 2 tbsp
- Cinnamon - 1 tsp
- Fresh lemon juice - 1 tbsp

DIRECTIONS:

1. Preheat the air fryer to 360 F/ 182 C.
2. Mix butter, lemon juice, sugar, and cinnamon in a bowl. Add peaches to the bowl and coat well.
3. Place peaches onto an airflow rack lined with parchment paper on the middle shelf of the air fryer and cook for 7 minutes.
4. Serve and enjoy.

Blueberry Cheese Muffins

PER SERVING:
CALORIES 415, CARBS 45G, FAT 23G, PROTEIN 7G

COOK TIME: 10 MINUTES
SERVES: 6
INGREDIENTS:

- Egg - 1
- Cream cheese, softened - 8 oz
- Olive oil - 1/4 cup
- Baking powder - 2 tsp
- Sugar - 1/2 cup
- All-purpose flour - 1 1/2 cups
- Blueberries - 1 cup
- Milk - 1/3 cup
- Vanilla - 1/2 tsp
- Salt - 1/2 tsp

DIRECTIONS:

1. Mix flour, sugar, baking powder, and salt in a bowl.
2. In a separate bowl, beat cream cheese, egg, vanilla, and oil.
3. Add milk and flour mixture and mix until well combined. Add blueberries and fold well.
4. Spoon batter into the greased muffin pan and place the pan on the middle shelf of the air fryer.
5. Cook muffins on air fryer mode at 320 F/ 160 C for 10 minutes.
6. Serve and enjoy.

Chocolate Pudding

PER SERVING:
CALORIES 510, CARBS 70G, FAT 27G, PROTEIN 7G

COOK TIME: 10 MINUTES
SERVES: 2
INGREDIENTS:

- Egg - 1
- All-purpose flour - 1/4 cup
- Cocoa powder - 1/3 cup
- Sugar - 1/2 cup
- Butter, melted - 1/4 cup
- Baking powder - 1/2 tsp

DIRECTIONS:

1. Mix flour, sugar, cocoa powder, and baking powder in a bowl.
2. Add egg and butter and stir until well combined.
3. Pour batter into the two greased ramekins and place the ramekins on the middle shelf of the air fryer.
4. Cook on air fry mode at 350 F/ 176 C for 10 minutes.
5. Serve and enjoy.

CONCLUSION

This epic cookbook contains 100 delicious recipes that will make you salivate just by reading them. You will understand and respect food better when you use this cookbook. Crispy fries and juicy chicken are no match for this book; there are also amazing dessert recipes. The Tower Xpress Air Fryer Oven Cookbook isn't just a collection of recipes. It is an invaluable resource that will help you understand the ins and outs of air frying. This cookbook will make your cooking experience more enjoyable and stress-free. It covers various recipe categories, from breakfast, lunch, and appetizers to desserts.

This page is for your notes

This page is for your notes

This page is for your notes

This page is for your notes